Spiritual Insights of T. W. Willingham

Book 9

Crumbs for the Would-Be Christlike

Crumbs for the Would-Be Christlike

Beacon Hill Press of Kansas City
Kansas City, Missouri

10 9 8 7 6 5 4 3 2 1

Contents

Foreword

Dr. T. W. Willingham is almost a legend in the Church of the Nazarene. He has served as pastor, district superintendent, college president, and executive at the world headquarters of the church.

Somewhat like Bernard Baruch he has been a close advisor to general superintendents and fledgling executive directors over the years. His business acumen and practical judgment have been sought after by all of us.

His greatest impact, however, has been in the spiritual realm. I and literally thousands have been stimulated by his insight into the Scriptures. Take these "crumbs," which I consider the most prophetic (prophetlike) pieces that have ever come from our presses, and revel in them.

—M. A. (BUD) LUNN

A Note of Thanks

First, I desire to thank my God for giving me time, strength, and guidance during the past 40 years as I have worked on the 16 books that I have had published.

In 1970, the Lord gave me a five-page directive concerning my writings in which He said, "I have given you two helpers . . . and it is My desire that they help you, and if they abide near Me they will feel the same way."

These two God-given workers—Clara Rogers and Kathy Butts—have been dependable and efficient and, more important, have felt that in so laboring they have been serving the Master and His kingdom.

Clara has corrected nearly all my handwritten articles, as well as typing many. Kathy has typed much, organized material, and by research and study, has made many valuable contributions. I thank God for both of them; without such help my work could not have been done.

If these messages prove to be of spiritual help to you, just give all the praise to our Heavenly Father.

—T. W. WILLINGHAM

Christ Could Not Save!

From childhood I have heard it preached with clarity and vehemence that Christ has power to save any and all— all that would come to Him. This has appeared to be the key note in most of the messages that I have heard from the pulpits. Written in bold letters on towering billboards and emblazoned with neon lights are the words "Jesus Saves." This claim is made for Him around the world. There is no major nation on earth that has not been told that this is true. Some have not believed it to be true, and some have in malice and hatred rejected it; nevertheless, its piercing echo has been heard around the world—"Jesus Saves."

But now comes our message—a message that is undeniably true: "Christ could not save." You may seek to refute it by much that is spoken and written of Him, yet the fact remains: He could not save. He made an effort to save, but gave it up. In fact, He prayed for the ability to save, but upon second thought, altered His petition.

What can or should we do with a would-be leader who could not save? Shall we dedicate our lives and eternal fortune to One of whom the inspired Word says, "He cannot save"?

There was a division here among His original followers. When those who claimed to be His most intimate and devoted followers saw that He could not save, they forsook Him and fled. "Why not?" they must have reasoned; "we have been looking for One who could save, and we had hopes that

9

we had found such an one in Christ—but alas! The naked truth is out; it can be hidden no longer—He can't save!"

Those were life's darkest hours for His followers. Some of them had forsaken fame and fortune to follow Him. They were living under the iron heel of Rome and were desperately in need of a deliverer. They had staked their all on this Stranger of Galilee. He had all the appearance of the Savior. He had shown signs again and again of His more-than-human insight, wisdom, and power. He had been able to still the troubled sea. His piercing replies had withered the wit and wisdom of the most shrewd lawyers. He had challenged the whole world and appeared to be its Conqueror. This was the verdict, evident and undeniable for many months—in fact, even years.

His followers dared to wager their all that He could outwit the wittiest, outshine the most brilliant, and lay His most relentless foes in the dirty dust. It was the joy of those who followed Him to believe this to be true; in fact, His bitterest foes had almost acknowledged defeat, and the whole countryside had come to hail Him as the great Savior. They hoped to crown Him king. His power, prestige, and performance gave unquestionable support to this decision. The vote was almost unanimous—He was the Savior.

In the crisis that would be decisive the fact was made clear; their high hopes were blasted—the dawn had quickly turned to dusk and to dark. All hope was gone. Despair seized the throne, fear filled their hearts, and their brilliant star had become a snuffed-out meteor. Their Savior could not save! They were right—He *could* not save! It is written in the Book of God: He tried, but He could not—He could not save!

If all this seems strange, it *is*—stranger than fiction. Fiction fades; facts endure. And this fact endures even to this day: we have a Savior who could not save! It was *himself* that He could not save!

In all of the darkness there was never a question as to

10

His ability to save others. No angel asked that question. The Father never questioned it. It was settled forever—He *could* save others, but himself He could not save.

Here the heart of the Redeemer is opened and the jewel of human redemption revealed. Only one could be saved—the Savior or the sinner. The Savior chose to save the sinner.

His followers should have known this. He had told them clearly that it was true: "Except a corn of wheat fall into the ground and die, it abideth alone: but if it die, it bringeth forth much fruit" (John 12:24). This had been His thesis from the very beginning, but they could not understand. This life born of death was an enigma to all of them. "Be it far from thee, Lord," cried Peter, but the Master responded, "Get thee behind me, Satan" (Matt. 16:22-23). The corn must die; death must precede life.

Professed Christians have been struggling in all ages over this central fact of life, that death must precede life. It seems so contrary to all of man's hopes and dreams. To live is the endless cry; to die one seldom hears. Only those who have faith dare to die, and "without faith it is impossible to please him" (Heb. 11:6). Death is the relinquishment of every hold on life in the belief that God is true and that He can bring life out of death. When this is firmly believed, death has no more sting. Why should it? It is dark and foreboding —"that last enemy" (1 Cor. 15:26)—but it is the portal to light and life.

The greatest need in Christendom today is life—the life of God—radiant, sparkling, and creative. There is just such life for everyone, but the process that leads to it is foreboding. We demand to see, but faith must outrun sight. The proof of it all must come from another, and that One has gone this way of death, and thence into life, and bids us follow.

With all the emphasis with which we have underscored His inability to save himself, we now, with even more emphasis, declare His ability to save all comers. His tent of grace is large enough to shelter every sin-sick soul, and His offer to do so is universal.

When He chose to die that others might live, Christ revealed the heart of His Father and made plain to all ages that the love of God reached past death into life eternal. This life from the ever-living Savior comes trooping back in His Spirit to enliven the hearts and hopes of all His followers. The death to which He invites us turns out to be a banquet of life, and the glow of His glory transmutes night shadows into the dawn of eternal day.

To die with Him has been His constant call through all the ages, but only those who have seen the daybreak beyond the darkness have heeded the call.

How may we persuade men to answer this death-life call? The answer is simple—live close enough to the risen Savior to radiate the glory of His presence. The world can only see it in us. No other medium is at hand. We must be the light-bearers; we have been appointed thereto. Is the light of our lives luminous? Does the path of our walking glow with His glory? If there were no other light but mine, could my neighbor find his way to glory? If this is a piercing question, it has fulfilled its mission. Our hearts must be stabbed into action—action that embodies all the force of our redeemed souls.

The dying of the Lord is not dying enough; His followers must follow Him in death, that the life and the resurrection may burst upon the sin-darkened world. Our lives, as His, must fall into the ground and die—die to the currents of worldly thinking, die to the hopes and sins of the masses, die to the high honors of men, die to self and all of its vanities. Yes, the call of death has been issued, and only those who answer its call can live.

To be alive, radiant, and happy after death is the most effective way to influence others to die. To die and remain dead is not desirable to man or to God; it is, therefore, the shouts of the morning after death that create the hunger for life that dawns upon death.

Christ trod no needless road, endured no useless agony, and points us to no unnecessary path. He calls only to the profitable, the blessed, the eternal; and He calls to death. Death, therefore, is the call to life. He answered that call and has been awarded a place at the Father's right hand. When He beckons us to follow, He calls us not to failure but to triumph. His death has become His eternal glory, and He desires that all mankind share that glory with Him; therefore, He calls to death as the only gateway into His presence.

He could not save himself, for He would save us. The corn of His soul fell into the ground to arise again in eternal fruitage, and He thus leads the way for each of us. That path has been tried; its bridges are safe, its hazards are well marked, and an experienced Guide has been sent to lead us. The dangers need not deter us, the bandits need not frighten us, and Satan himself cannot defeat us. Up, then, my timid friend, and brave the path that the saints have trod! There are footprints all the way—the same that marked the shores of Galilee and were to be seen beside the leper's hut. They lead from earth to heaven by the way of death, life, and eternal rest. Press on, my friends, press on!

Sifting for the Gold

I was intrigued by the sifting, panning process of a father and his son as they sought the precious metal in the bed of Cripple Creek, Colo. Day after day—in fact, year after year—they had searched for the gold midst the sands of that beautiful stream. Not more than once in a thousand pans of silt did they find a precious nugget, but when found, the search became well worthwhile.

Only for a few hours have I panned for the gold that perisheth, but for more than half a century have I sought for the "gold tried in the fire" (Rev. 3:18). Admittedly, it is hard to come by. The Word confirms this, enjoining us to seek "her as silver" (Prov. 2:4). The total potential of human personality must be used to secure the best that God has in store for one.

During a lifetime, or even within a single year, there come to the mind hundreds, even thousands, of thoughts, ideas, and suggestions from various sources, some of them demanding immediate attention, some of them strange and uncanny, some with a beautiful aura, some in tatters and rags. Occasionally one is clearly from beneath, for it bears the indelible stamp of Satan; at times one comes as a quiet, scripturally backed word from God.

If all the thoughts were clearly marked and the badge that they carried represented their true nature, the selection would be easy; but alas! that is not always the case. Packages of stones are marked "Food." Poisons are marked "Medicine." The glittering glass is marked "diamonds," and the flakes of fool's gold are labeled "gold."

To further deceive the searcher, the messengers bearing the parcels are at times traitors and deceivers. True angels come bearing messages of hope and orders for service, but angels of darkness come clothed as "angels of light" (see 2 Cor. 11:14), bearing messages that appear to be genuine and heaven-sent. It would be wonderful if all things were as they seem, but that is not the case.

If one would find the gold of God, he must search among the sands; and if he would hear the Voice from above, he must be able to distinguish it from the medley of voices bearing down upon him.

This picture of the needed diligence of the seeker has not been overdrawn. The Word substantiates the basic facts herein set forth. We are told of the deceivers who would "deceive the very elect," if possible (Matt. 24:24). We are also told that many will arrive at the scene of judgment disappointed and condemned, when all the while they believed that all was well with them. So sure will they be of their salvation that they will argue with the Judge as to the justice of His verdict.

We have been alerted to the danger of being deceived, and are warned, "Be not deceived." There is hope in this warning, for what God commands, He is able and willing, even anxious, to help us to perform. It remains, therefore, for us to employ the means that God has placed at our disposal, and to be guided by the Guide whom He has sent to pilot us through.

Although there are dangers, numerous and deadly, there is absolute safety for one who will follow the Guide. He knows the value and nature of every pebble and the identity of every speaking voice, and He stands ready to instruct and guide all who will heed His voice.

How, then, may one be assured of His assistance? What qualities of soul are prerequisite to His leading? At the very top of the list we would put the necessity of being like Him in

15

spirit. We are reminded that two cannot "walk together, except they be agreed" (Amos 3:3). Our spirit, therefore, must be like His, and His Spirit is one of meekness and lowliness that issues in "rest" (Matt. 11:28-29).

One cannot be sure of the voice that is speaking when his soul is not at rest. The Spirit leads in the atmosphere of His own being, and that atmosphere is calm. He is not disturbable and does not speak from an agitated nature. The calm of His being would speak to the calm of ours, and until ours is calmed by coming to Him, He cannot speak to us. It is to the meek and lowly that the peace-giving message from the Spirit comes. Agitation must cease; if it does not, then heed not the speaker. When God speaks and we heed, there is calm, and the path becomes clear. The dross of our thinking can be separated from the gold of His message, and our enriched soul will be on its happy way.

The second prerequisite to the guidance of the Spirit is the sharing of His purpose. There is no question as to His purpose. The One who sent Him declared it: "He shall glorify me" (John 16:14). There is nothing of value in thought or in action that does not redound to the glory of Christ. For us, He must be central and His honor paramount.

If, in our seeking, our spirit is feverish and our minds confused, we should just relax and commit all to His care; and if our surrender and commitment is complete, His guidance is guaranteed. "The meek will he guide in judgment: and the meek will he teach his way" (Ps. 25:9).

If there is a quiet, relaxed, and committed soul doing the searching, the gold can be distinguished from the glittering sands. The voice of the angel can be discerned, and the voice of the deceiver rejected.

If we have emphasized the dangers of deception, with equal emphasis and more, we assure the searcher's success if the clearly announced rules are obeyed and the heaven-sent Guide followed.

16

I Do Not Understand;
I Need Not

The apostle Paul leaves us this very encouraging message: "If any man think that he knoweth any thing, he knoweth nothing yet as he ought to know" (1 Cor. 8:2). In another place, it is recorded that "we know in part" (13:9).

These messages are very comforting and in full accord with my condition. More wonderful still is the fact that I don't need to know. There are great theological questions that I cannot answer; there are statements in accepted creeds that I do not understand.

I often puzzle my friends when I say that I can't accept some things, for I do not understand them to be true. It is painful to think honestly. It is much easier to profess beliefs just because great men of one's school have affirmed them. One need not deny what he cannot understand, but it is mental folly to declare belief when one has no personal certainty in the matter.

None of my ignorance and half knowledge disturbs me greatly. I am ever searching for truth, and for the deeper meaning in all truths. But I find that to profess belief in that which others accept as true, without understanding it myself, is one of the greatest barriers to understanding that there is.

It is better for one to acknowledge ignorance and hold the profession of belief in abeyance at the expense of criticism, than to claim belief when there is no certain ground for it known to him. A wholesome ignorance confessed is far better than the profession of a belief for which one has no foundation.

It is not necessary to understand all that others say they understand. It is highly desirable to know, know more, know all that one can know; but it is no disgrace to admit, "I don't know," when that is true. This opens the door for light and understanding. No one will invite you to eat when you have just eaten, nor to understand what you claim you already know.

It is the glib profession of knowledge in so many areas of scriptural truth where there is no such knowledge that causes us to remain in ignorance. Truth will lead to truth. Honesty opens the door for light.

There are a number of areas of biblical teaching that I do not understand. Take the matter of "election"; here is a doctrine that separates two great schools of thought, the Arminian and Calvinist. I have never tried to preach on this subject, for I do not understand it. I can use many of the arguments of my school in support of our conclusions, but I cannot honestly say that I can answer the arguments given by those who disagree with our position.

My mind rests better by not attempting to prove what I do not understand, and by not condemning what I am not sure is untrue. I keep an ignorant but open mind on the subject matter. I have been encouraged to do so by the uncertainty of some who profess certainty, but who, upon cross-examination, must rely upon the quotations of others when they have no answer of their own.

Likewise, I do not understand the Trinity, and I rejoice that one as ignorant as I can make it to heaven without this knowledge. Even the wisest do not profess to know it all at this point, for the finite mind can never fully understand or comprehend the Infinite, but I have not been able to understand what some seem to see so clearly. To confess ignorance is to open the way for light. This I am glad to do.

I do not understand the preincarnate nature of Christ, and the portion that appears most clear to me is not in harmony with the view of many of my contemporaries. To accept as true some of their beliefs would destroy my faith in Christ as a Savior. In such a case, I hold to Him as my Redeemer, and expect to understand Him more fully by and by.

I cannot harmonize the foreknowledge of God and free moral agency; some of my friends seem to be able to do so. Again, for me to accept their thinking would wreck my faith in God, so I hold to my faith that saves me (of that I am sure); to know more fully will come later if I stay saved.

I do not understand how Jesus Christ, who arose and ascended as a tangible, visible person can dwell in my heart. If the answer is that He does so by His Spirit, I still plead ignorance. How can He speak to me and to a million others at the same time, and on different subjects? How can He share my joys and the joys of a thousand others at the same time, and enter into the sorrows of an equal number all in the same moment of time? How can this be? The only adequate answer is, "I do not know."

I do not know how my invisible, intangible self can leave this mortal body at the end of life's day and carry with it all that is of value in my life. How large is my soul? Of what substance is it made? Where is my spirit? Will my spirit and my soul be separated? I have heard some answers to such questions, but in spite of all the answers I still say, "I don't know."

When I speak frankly, I must confess that I know but little, and know that little imperfectly. That is what Paul is trying to tell us.

I am gazing upon my miniature garden from my study window. There are roses, raspberries, strawberries, grapes, onions, lettuce, radishes, rhubarb, mangoes, and turnips, with grass and weeds. How does the raspberry gather blackness from the air, rain, and soil, for its ripened fruit, while the

19

strawberry gathers red for its decoration? Just how is it that the roots of the onion search out the strong odor from the soil, while the roots of the rose find the fragrance of the scented rosebud? Yes, I am not ignorant of some of the answers to these queries, but having heard them, I must again answer, "I do not understand."

How can the invisible atom carry the heat to melt steel beams and power to destroy a whole city? I hear that this is true, but why? That I cannot answer.

Reams of paper could be employed to catalog the things that I do not know and that I can never know in time. Why then should I demand knowledge of the nature and attributes of the Infinite?

Long since, I have given to reason (the god of the years of my atheism) a backseat and placed love and faith in the driver's seat. I have not dethroned reason; it is valuable. God asks us to use it—use it in dealing with men and with himself. "Come now, and let us reason together, saith the Lord" (Isa. 1:18). But its throne is miniature; it rides in the rear while love and faith guide us onward.

Advice that I have given college students is fitting here: "Park your heads in the hedge at the door, and bring your hearts to the altar in total consecration; then walk out and pick up a good head and use it the rest of your life." Good advice, if I did give it!

Reason must be taken from the driver's seat, and faith installed. In fact, a soul might be saved without reason, for the way is so plain that "wayfaring men, though fools, shall not err therein" (Isa. 35:8); "But without faith it is impossible to please him" (Heb. 11:6).

In the light of all this, I do not unchristianize myself or others for not knowing all that some think we must know to be Christians. One can make it through to God and heaven if he can say with the restored blind man, "One thing I know, that, whereas I was blind, now I see" (John 9:25). Faith, and not knowledge, saves us.

The Approach

The approach is important. Its importance is determined by the nature of the object being approached. The improper approach of a motorist to a narrow bridge could spell his death. The pilot's wrong approach to the runway could mean tragedy for 100 lives. The wrong approach of a salesman could mean the loss of a sale. The losses in such cases, though great, are not all-important; they involve only money or human lives.

The all-important object of approach is God, the supreme and eternal. The approach to Him is, therefore, the all-important approach. We are not left in darkness as to how we should approach Him. "He that cometh to God must believe that he is" (Heb. 11:6). It is self-evident that one could not or would not seek to approach a nonexistent being. But it is not enough for one to believe that God exists; he must realize that Christ is the only door that opens into the heart of God. "I am the door"; all that climb up another way are thieves and robbers (John 10:7-8). It therefore becomes necessary for one to know how to approach the Door. As one must believe in God if he is to find Him, so in like faith must one approach the Door; hence the command, "Ye believe in God, believe also in me" (14:1).

With firm belief that God is, and an equally firm belief that Christ is the only door through which one may enter into the heart of God, the right approach to Christ is all-important.

How then may I approach Him? There are many ave-

21

nues of approach to Him, one of which is through the written Word. Jesus declared concerning the Scriptures, "They are they which testify of me" (John 5:39). How then must one approach this testimony concerning Him, and how may its message be understood?

First: I believe that the written Word is God's message, inspired by God Himself. The only valid attitude of approach is the heartfelt affirmation that "all scripture is given by inspiration of God, and is profitable" (2 Tim. 3:16). Without seeking to verify this statement, I approach the written Word in the assurance that it is true.

Second: I believe (and must) that God knew what He was writing about—that His thoughts were clearly known to Him, and that all that He said at one time is consistent with other things that He said at other times and through other penmen.

Third: I believe that God's recollection of all that He has caused to be written is perfect. He has in mind now all that He ever inspired and the purpose that He had in mind when He inspired it.

Fourth: I believe that since this divine revelation has come to us on earth, that its understanding is meant for us. It has been spoken that it might be understood, and preserved because it bears a message for us all. This fact is confirmed in Deut. 29:29, "The secret things belong unto the Lord our God: but those things which are revealed belong unto us and to our children for ever, that we may do all the words of this law."

Fifth: I believe that one must have some assistance in understanding this message. The Word affirms this, and God has promised such helpers. "When he ascended up on high . . . he gave some . . . teachers" (Eph. 4:8, 11). How may one learn except he be taught? The divinely called teacher is therefore important.

But more important than earthly teachers is the Christ-sent Teacher, the Holy Spirit. "They shall be all taught of God" (John 6:45) is a promise to all who will enter the school of the Highest. The divinely appointed teachers, like the law of the Old Testament, are our schoolmasters ever leading us to the Master Teacher, who alone can lead us into Christ.

The teaching, therefore, of all human teachers is relative and not absolute. It becomes absolute and final when it is in perfect accord with the teachings of the Great Teacher. For this reason, no one can safely anchor his faith to teachings of any man or any school of thought, or any creed worked out by any council.

The liberated soul, the soul set free in Christ, evaluates all sermons of men and findings of churches and councils in the light of the revelation of "the truth [as it] is in Jesus" (Eph. 4:21); for it is only "in the face of Jesus Christ" that "the light of the . . . glory of God" can be seen (2 Cor. 4:6), and only the Great Teacher, the Holy Spirit, can make clear that revelation.

To be an accredited scholar in the school of the Spirit, at least five things are necessary:

First: One must have a passionate desire to know the Truth, the Truth himself. There are many, many references to this necessary passion for truth in both Testaments. Prov. 2:1-9 is a full-orbed expression of it. One must cry after knowledge, seek her as silver, search for her as for hidden treasure. The Psalmist voices such a desire on many occasions, such as in Psalm 119: "I cried with my whole heart"; "I prevented the dawning of the morning, and cried"; and "With my whole heart have I sought thee" (vv. 145, 147, 10). Such seeking was accompanied with his promise, "Give me understanding, and I shall keep thy law" (v. 34). Having thus sought and promised, he could affirm, "Thou hast taught me" and in exultation proclaim, "I rejoice at thy word, as one that findeth great spoil" (vv. 102, 162).

Second: One must be pledged to obey the truth. "I have chosen the way of truth" (Ps. 119:30) must be his abiding purpose, for the promise is "If any man will do his will, he shall know" (John 7:17).

Third: One must put all earthly teachers on a secondary basis. Christ must be the final court of appeal. The apostle Paul exhorted the Corinthians, "Be ye followers of me" (1 Cor. 4:16). He repeated the exhortation to the Philippian brethren (Phil. 3:17), assuring them that in so doing "the God of peace shall be with you" (4:9), but he made it clear that their following should be checked by Christ. "Be ye followers of me, even as I also am of Christ" (1 Cor. 11:1) was his final word. The human leader could not be the final authority. This the apostle recognized and practiced. He began his ministerial career in a personal encounter with God and pursued it under the direction of His Spirit. He puts it this way: "But when it pleased God . . . to reveal his Son in me . . . I conferred not with flesh and blood: neither went I up to Jerusalem to them which were apostles before me" (Gal. 1:15-17). He had a high regard for the brethren, but Jesus Christ was his final appeal. One is never free until he is anchored in Christ so completely that he can stand if all else gives way.

Fourth: One must believe in and accept the instructions of the Great Teacher. Christ promised that the Holy Spirit would guide us into all truth, but a guide is useless unless we will follow.

Fifth: One must bear the personal responsibility of deciding what the teaching of God is. If he is to be guided by others, finally guided, by what group must he be guided? My group says by the Arminian school; others say we must be guided by the Calvinist; on and on, the conflicting demands come flooding in. Here it must be said, "Let every man be fully persuaded in his own mind" (Rom. 14:5). Since this is true, the message of Paul takes on meaning of great im-

24

portance: "Work out your own salvation with fear and trembling" (Phil. 2:12).

As fearful and as breathtaking as the task is, I must assume it; no other can. I must determine what is God's path for me in the light of His written Word and the leadership of the Holy Spirit. My conclusions should be checked by others who seek the right way, but the final decision as to the right path is mine, and mine alone. On this basis and no other may I be asked to bear the final verdict in the day of judgment.

If It Die

(John 12:24)

Here again, a small word is very significant. The word "if" marks the division between barrenness and fruitfulness. "If it die, it bringeth forth much fruit"; "Except . . . [it] die, it abideth alone" (John 12:24).

It takes faith to die, but that is the only route for fruitfulness. Our religion is first an experience of death, and then one of life. The order is correct: death-life. The order cannot be changed, for death is temporary, while life is eternal. We die in order to live.

When Jesus was speaking of the corn of wheat dying, He was speaking of himself. He knew that His life would be forever barren unless He died. He could only save by His death. This He knew well and came to die for sinners. Their life was bound up in His death. He must die to save; there was no other way.

Since by His death alone could sin be removed, the enemy sought to get Him to bypass the Cross and accept the kingdoms of the world at his hands without death. The devil later used Peter as a mouthpiece, but Jesus said to them both—for they were of the same spirit—"Get thee behind me, Satan" (Matt. 16:23; Mark 8:33). He was thus declaring the necessity of the seed-corn's death as the road to its fruitfulness.

The death of Christ is a pattern for our death. He has invited us to follow Him, bearing our cross, the symbol of our oneness with Him.

The thought of death is not a pleasant one; it is therefore accompanied with the promise of success. "If it die, it bringeth forth much fruit." The dark alternative is presented also. "Except . . . [it] die, it abideth alone." In the light of these two alternatives, man must make his decision; sterility or fruitfulness—take your choice.

What is the nature and extent of the fruitfulness of the Master's death? Upon it hung the eternal salvation of the saints of the past, the followers of His day, and the souls of all who were to come.

His death would make possible a host of redeemed souls who would be present through all eternity to sing His praises, and to give witness to the angels of the extent of God's love for sinners—a love that was willing to die. He died and saw "the travail of his soul, and [was] satisfied" (Isa. 53:11). This was the joy that was set before Him that enabled Him to endure the Cross and despise its shame. The end was ever in His thinking, and it lured Him onward.

If, on the other hand, He had chosen not to die, He would have returned to His Father (if return He could) empty-handed. There would be no shouts of redeemed souls from any age. The due bills for redemption given to Abraham, David, the thief on the cross, and all others would be canceled. Paul makes this perfectly clear in the 15th chapter of 1 Corinthians. The death of Christ was necessary to preserve the integrity of God and to populate heaven with the redeemed.

Could Christ let the Father down? disgrace Him before the angels? annul all His promises and stamp Him as a deceiver? No, never! The price was too great. He chose to die and prove His love and the love of the Father. The integrity of both the Father and the Son were at stake. Christ would not fail; His eternal kingdom depended upon it. He would not fail; He did not. Praise His wonderful name forever!

This dying corn of wheat has meaning for His followers

also. We, too, who care to follow Him must die or abide alone. His death symbolizes the spiritual process that we must follow if we are to go with Him. Our religion must be one of death before it can become one of life. Here comes the test. Are we willing to die—die with Him?

Even death becomes glorious when entered into in Him, and that is the way of the Christian death. We are buried with Him "in the likeness of his death" (Rom. 6:5). When thus buried, we have the assurance of sharing the resurrection with Him, and a seat with Him in the heavenlies. The joy set before Him enabled Him to endure the Cross; likewise, it is the joy set before us of a crown of glory and eternal rest that strengthens us in this participation in His death.

Another incentive is the reward for service and soul winning. We are promised that "they that turn many to righteousness [shall shine] as the stars for ever and ever" (Dan. 12:3). This is not a passing flash of recognition but an eternal reward. No wonder Paul remarked that "our light affliction, which is but for a moment, worketh for us a far more exceeding and eternal weight of glory" (2 Cor. 4:17).

Death is not a sacrifice; it is an investment, an investment that will pay eternal dividends of joy, treasure, and eternal companionship.

The alternative to death is barrenness, and more than barrenness, lostness. The blackness of the darkness awaits those who choose rather to live in death than to die that they may live forever.

The glorious thing about this death-life process is that Christ went through it in the presence of a great multitude, and arose again and revealed himself to hundreds of His followers by "many infallible proofs" (Acts 1:3). Thus doing, He delivered "them who through fear of death were all their lifetime subject to bondage" (Heb. 2:15). Our religion, therefore, is one of life and not of death. Death is only the portal to life.

When we die with Him, we are raised with Him by the same power that raised Him—the infinite power of the Father. Thereafter, we sit in the heavenlies with Him and await His coming again.

In the light of all the facts, what is the verdict? What is our purpose? I don't know about yours, but I feel as did Joshua of old: "But as for me and my house, we will serve the Lord" (Josh. 24:15).

The testimony of one very reliable witness who made a great sacrifice to go this way is, "I count all things but loss for . . . Christ Jesus my Lord: for whom I have suffered the loss of all things, and do count them but dung, that I may win Christ" (Phil. 3:8). Dissatisfied customers don't speak that way, and Christ has no dissatisfied customers. If one is dissatisfied, he has not as yet been crucified with Christ and raised with Him. There is no disappointment among His followers, only among those who profess but do not possess. Christians are happy people.

Sin—Occasional, and as a Pattern of Life

The theological gunfire has been ceaseless over the subject of sin. Does the sanctified Christian sin, or not? That seems to be the issue.

A part of the difficulty —but by no means all—is eliminated when each contender defines his terms. Certainly one who lives in constant known disobedience to the will of God—thus sinning—cannot be Christian; but is there a difference between an occasional sin and a set pattern of sin, and may the Christian fall at times into the former?

The perfectionist group definitely rejects any act that may be characterized by the word "sin" as having any place in the life of a Christian. "He that committeth sin is of the devil" (1 John 3:8); "Whosoever abideth in him sinneth not: whosoever sinneth hath not seen him, neither known him" (v. 6)—and many other such scriptures form the basis for their position.

Others reason that there is a difference between a sudden act of sin and a reasoned commitment to a life of sin. If one follows the reasoning of the perfectionist, there are certain statements in the Word of God that must be harmonized with their position.

Because of this conflict over this unresolved issue, the perfectionist groups use Matthew's version of the Lord's Prayer, which contains the phrase "forgive us our debts," almost exclusively, and reject Luke's "forgive us our sins." In so

30

doing, there seems to be an unwillingness to face the whole issue of sin frankly and fully. There is no reasonable doubt but that these two recordings are an attempt to quote Jesus accurately. It is possible that this was a prayer admonition repeated many times by Jesus himself, and in some instances the word "sin" was used, and in others, the word "debt." Be that as it may, the word "sins" does occur in this portion of the Word of God and as having come from the lips of Jesus himself. Is it therefore to be frowned upon because it contradicts some well-established teaching of a certain group, be it ever so large?

Without reasonable doubt, this prayer was taught to His disciples as indicated in the text, and whatever they were taught to pray for must have been, or could have been, a reality in their lives and in the lives of other disciples in the days following.

There is also no question about the meaning of the word "sins" as thus used. It is the same word that is used in the following passages where the meaning is generally accepted at face value.

Just before Christ ascended to the Father, He commanded "that repentance and remission of sins should be preached in his name among all nations" (Luke 24:47).

The apostle Paul, following this command, writes, "For I delivered unto you first of all that which I also received, how that Christ died for our sins according to the scriptures" (1 Cor. 15:3).

John continues, "But if we walk in the light, as he is in the light, we have fellowship one with another, and the blood of Jesus Christ his Son cleanseth us from all sin" (1 John 1:7).

Again John writes, "If any man see his brother sin a sin which is not unto death, he shall ask, and he shall give him life for them that sin not unto death. There is a sin unto death: I do not say that he shall pray for it. All unrighteousness is sin: and there is a sin not unto death" (1 John 5:16-17).

James, commenting on the same subject, writes, "Then when lust hath conceived, it bringeth forth sin: and sin, when it is finished, bringeth forth death" (James 1:15).

It is needless to quote more passages in which the subject of sin is dealt with. It is noteworthy that the word translated "sin" in each of the above cases is from the same Greek word.

Herein the statement is made that there is a sin "which is not unto death." It is stated elsewhere, "The soul that sinneth, it shall die" (Ezek. 18:4). Is God trying to say to us that there is a difference between the single act of sin and a commitment to a life of sin, and that the former may be committed at times by the truly Christian, confessed and immediately covered by the Blood, and the connection with the Savior be not terminated?

Then, too, there is the statement concerning the Advocate of which the Christian has been assured. John addressed his message to "little children" and reminded them that "if any man sin, we have an advocate with the Father, Jesus Christ the righteous: And he is the propitiation for our sins" (1 John 2:1-2).

This seems to imply that the little children would be sinning at times, and he wanted them to know that provision had been made to take care of their sins.

Would it not be more scriptural—and hence wiser—to allow that Christians do sin at time and may turn immediately for forgiveness to the Advocate, than to make a single act of "sin" to completely break the connection of the soul with God? This position would allow for the ministry of chastening, the use of the Advocate, and the acceptance of the Lord's Prayer as recorded by Luke, which prayer is now virtually taboo with the perfectionist.

Aside from the Word of God, there is a practical consideration that thrusts itself upon one who has listened to holiness preachers for so long, and it is a somewhat disturbing element. I speak of the spirit that is so often felt to be present in preaching on this subject. Seldom have I felt a spirit of humility and of meekness on the part of the minister when discussing the viewpoint of the other side. I know there is no place for toleration of false doctrine, but there is the commandment, "The servant of the Lord must not strive; but be gentle unto all men, apt to teach, patient, in meekness instructing those that oppose themselves; if God peradventure will give them repentance to the acknowledging of the truth" (2 Tim. 2:24-25).

There is another very disturbing fact that I have observed across the years in the lives of holiness people in general, and that is an almost universal unwillingness to forgive the backslider and to forget. This is especially true of a minister who has fallen. My connections in the church, which for well over half a century have brought me face-to-face with this problem, have compelled me to give it some thought. I am thoroughly convinced that Jesus Christ would not take the same attitude toward a penitent minister who had fallen as is generally taken by our own church. I feel this so strongly that I thoughtfully say, If I thought Christ would take such an attitude, I would still be looking for a Savior. It is not the picture of the One I serve and call Lord.

I hasten to add that because of our own weakness, we are unable to deal with such as Christ would. It would be like a young convert trying to steady a wobbling saint. Such tasks are reserved for the spiritual. Paul elucidates this very clearly when advising them how to restore the fallen among them: "Ye which are spiritual, restore such an one in the spirit of meekness" (Gal. 6:1).

The fact that we are too weak to be Christlike does not disturb me so much as the fact that we attribute our weakness to our holiness, and glory in it rather than lament it, and fail to seek to grow up. It would appear that this particular problem grows out of the claim to a perfection that we do not

33

possess, and that an attitude of perfect honesty, humility, and confession would help us to grow into maturity more rapidly.

The rebuttal to my reasoning or opinion at this point is well known to me. The answer is: A minister who falls into social sin is likely to do the same again and is therefore unsafe.

To this I reply: There is something about forgiveness, when genuinely given, that has a powerful influence in the repentant sinner's life to keep him from falling. On the other hand, if he is held at arm's length, he must make it back, not only with the opposition of the devil but also with the additional millstone of unforgiveness that we hang about his neck.

I reemphasize what I believe to be generally true—we have overappraised our righteousness and steadfastness and have felt that we are above the weak brother who has fallen but is striving to get back. It seems that our look is more that of disdain than of "considering thyself, lest thou also be tempted" (Gal. 6:1).

In this same connection, it must be remembered what Jesus said to Peter on the subject of forgiveness many years ago. Peter wanted to know just how far he needed to go in this matter of forgiveness. He posed the perfect number 7 as being the limit. Jesus multiplied that by 70 and handed it back to Peter. It was then that Peter asked for an increase in faith. Such a prayer well becomes us.

There is another observation that I have made in this field. I have watched those that have been so merciless on those that they considered had sinned. It is from this group that a large number of casualties has come. There is a law written, "Blessed are the merciful: for they shall obtain mercy" (Matt. 5:7). That law is still effective.

The attitude generally taken by us is that time is necessary to prove one who has fallen and has been forgiven. Can you feature Jesus saying to Peter as He stood with the group in the hour of ascension and was commissioning them to go out to preach—"Now, Peter, you will remember that only a few days ago you denied Me and swore that you never knew Me. I want you to keep out of the ministry for at least two years, and if you have then proven yourself to be true, we will send you to a home mission charge"!

But someone will answer, That is different. Here is a minister who has sinned against a woman.

Yes, I know that is different. His sin was great. It was against a woman, and of course, that is much worse than a sin against the little Jesus—for after all, that doesn't count for much anyway!

No, these are not the words of the answer; but alas! too often I fear it represents the real attitude.

The above is not to be construed as a defense of a sinning religion, but it is an honest effort to harmonize various statements in the Word of God on the subject of sin.

There is no point in trying to ignore reality, and there is no virtue in having a closed mind to truth. If certain other truths do not seem to harmonize with our doctrine, then we should examine them in the honesty of an oncoming judgment. One cannot be blamed justly for trying to face the Word of God honestly. I think several of our younger ministers have been lost to the church by the unwillingness or inability of some of their seniors to face their questions honestly, even if they should have to painfully admit that there were some things that they did not know.

Only as one is honest with himself, with others, and with God can he hope to receive or to give much help.

I Have Heard the Thunder; I Would Hear the Voice

In the 12th chapter of John's Gospel is the record of one of the Master's public prayers; and when He had finished, there came a clear "voice from heaven," giving assurance that His prayer had been heard. He said that this Voice did not come for His benefit but for the benefit of those that "stood by"; so we must find in the reactions of the bystanders the lessons to be learned through the Voice from above.

Standing there were three classes of hearers, and they all heard. There was Jesus in the center; to Him the voice was clear, its message understandable. Near Him were those who also heard; they knew not the source of the message nor its content, but they did believe it was from above: "An angel spake to him," they said. Further out were those who heard; to them it was but thunder—superhuman but unintelligible.

It seems that Jesus was trying to tell us that there are three classes who hear from above: himself, to whom the message is clear and meaningful; others who sense its meaningfulness but cannot grasp it; and still others who hear, but the hearing brings no sense of meaning—it is from above but does nothing but attract attention.

I thank God for the thunder. I have spent much time where that was all I heard; but I thank God for it, for it attracted my attention, and that is the first step toward God. It was

36

the flaming bush that attracted Moses' attention; and it was when he turned aside to see, that "God called unto him out of the midst of the bush" (Exod. 3:4). Too often we are so far removed from the center of the descending Voice that it is to us but thunder; and if we heed not the thunder, turn not aside to see, draw no closer to the Master, there will be no Voice, clear and understandable.

In Mark 6 there is an interesting story illustrating how Jesus would become real to us. The disciples were at sea in a storm "toiling in rowing." Like rumbling thunder with no clear message, Jesus walked along as vague reality: "They supposed it had been a spirit." But like an inquiring Moses at the bush, they "cried out." Then came the clear vision of the Master, the "Be of good cheer: it is I; be not afraid," and the ceasing of the wind. Their amazement and wonder remained, but the miracle that saved them was real, and the Master who performed it was made known to them. The significant, and yet almost unbelievable, fact of the story is that He "would have passed by them (vv. 47-51).

The lesson that we must learn is that if we heed not His voice, although so far away it seems to us but thunder, and turn not to see the phenomenon of the bush, nor "cry out" at the sight of the ghostly spirit, there will be no revelation of the divine message nor the God who proclaims it.

So important is it that we heed the faintest whisper, that this truth is further illustrated by the story of the two brethren on the road to Emmaus and the Stranger who joined them with a message that caused their hearts to burn. Again there is the significant fact that "he made as though he would have gone further" (Luke 24:28). They constrained Him to come in; then came His self-revelation. His message and presence burns our hearts, but His self-revealing is determined by our constraint for His abiding.

I humbly but frankly confess that I spend much of my time at such a distance from the One who lived always in the circle of the Father's clear voice, that I hear but thunder, and so often have I heeded it not. I have turned not aside to see. I have raised no cry to the unknown, and urged not the Stranger to abide with me.

This is a painful confession, but may it be that through the suffering, I may learn a better obedience. By God's grace, it shall be so. While this confession is mine, it could and should be made by many of my friends. Many times it has been said to me by troubled friends, "I have had a strange feeling about that. Do you think God is trying to say something to me?" My answer: "It could be, and if attention is given, He will reveal himself if He is there."

I shall be the first to confess that my oft abode in the realm of the thunder is not God's appointed best for my life. Too often and too much have I moved in the permissible second best, rather than in the path of His first choice. To deny this would be to lie; and to fail to confess it would be to close the door to forgiveness and possible improvement.

Perhaps the most prolific cause of our drifting from the center, where the hearing is clear and understandable, is set forth by Jesus as "the cares of this world, and the deceitfulness of riches, and the lust of other things" (Mark 4:19). Man's affections drift so easily from the "things which are above" (Col. 3:1) to the trivial toys of times, and the glamor of the fleeting so quickly eclipses the glory of the eternal.

Jesus enjoined us to strive to "enter . . . in at the strait gate" (Matt. 7:13), and eternal vigilance is required, lest the broad way become our choosing. The throng has its influence, and its empty laughter can soon come to be mistaken for "the blessing of the Lord . . . [which] maketh rich, and he addeth no sorrow with it" (Prov. 10:22).

Jesus was warning us of the bane of desiring things, for things perish and so does the soul that is attached to them; hence the index finger of the Master ever pointing to the "things which are above." The viewpoint of the Master can be seen only as we stand close by His side. The clarity of the voice becomes ours only when we move from the region of the thunder to the companionship of the Son. There are unfilled seats by His side, and He calls, "Come unto me . . . and learn . . . and . . . find rest unto your souls. For my yoke is easy, and my burden is light" (Matt. 11:28-30).

I Conferred Not with Flesh and Blood

(Gal. 1:16)

We are living in a day of conferences. As soon as a problem arises, we set up a conference. The conference rooms are among the most important items in a well-organized business. The president, mayors, governors, unions—just name it and we will add it—nearly everybody, it seems, is just coming from or going to a conference.

Conferences have their place. They must not be ruled out completely. There the ingredients of many minds combine to produce an edible loaf. It might be said that Christ held conferences with His disciples at times, so they have their place.

The apostle Paul began his career with a conference, perhaps of some length. The unique feature of his conference was that it was not of the normal kind; it was rare indeed—flesh and blood were excluded. It was a conference nonetheless, perhaps one of the world's most valuable ones. It was patterned after the practice of the Master, who went alone to the mountain for conference with the Father. Jesus advocated this kind of conference for His followers. It is the conference of the shut door.

Paul began his ministry on this high level. May we suggest some reasons why the apostle began his work with this high-level conference.

First: He had met a speaking Lord. He had had a God all along—a God who "spake unto Moses" (John 9:29)—but never before had he met a God who could speak to Paul in the Hebrew language. This was an experience that was "out of this world," and he wanted to extend this conference that had begun on the Damascus road.

Second: The conversation begun on the road was a personal one, and it was not necessary—not even desirable—that the size of the conference be enlarged. He was the only one that needed to know what was to be discussed; hence, he conferred with no other.

Third: The unusual nature of the subject matter to be discussed was not for the larger group. Paul was to get a "revelation of the mystery, which was kept secret since the world began" (Rom. 16:25). God was to draw aside the hiding veil and allow the new convert to see what angels had desired to look into but were denied that privilege. Such revelations are seldom given to a committee.

Then, too, Paul was to be told of the things that he must suffer for the cause of Christ, and he could best hear such things alone with his God.

Fourth: Paul was not immediately received by the other leaders, and a conference with a larger group would probably have caused some disturbance and disagreement. God could deal with him alone better than in a large group.

Fifth: Perhaps the controlling motive that caused the apostle to pass up all others and be alone with his God grew out of his very constitution. Paul was a man who wanted things straight and firsthand. He wanted to speak with power and finality, he knew that there was but one final Source of authority, and he wanted to come into long and vital contact with that Source.

Had he received his message from men, they could conceivably have changed the message, as indeed, some did; so he wanted to get it firsthand. He fairly boasts in his letter to

41

the church at Galatia, "But I certify you, brethren, that the gospel which was preached of me is not after man . . . but by the revelation of Jesus Christ" (Gal. 1:11-12).

Having received his message in the closed conference room with his Lord, he could face all the errors that might arise and declare that if "an angel from heaven, preach any other gospel unto you . . . let him be accursed" (v. 8). One does not get such certainty from a council, conference, or committee.

Nothing short of a revelation from God to one's own heart can put such certainty behind the truth. Paul must find finality in God, and in God alone. The time came when all Asia turned against him, and no one stood with him. Here he needed to find finality in the One who is finality. He found it alone with Him.

Certainly we would not argue that the apostle is in every respect a pattern for us. He received initial insights that were his alone. Many of his experiences have not been the lot of the masses, and some of none other, and yet there are some experiences in his conference alone that all should share.

First: There must be an intimate personal meeting with the Savior. No one can share this experience with us. They may be present and enjoy the overflow, but there is a secret retreat of the soul where one meets with his Redeemer alone. God has no duplicate fingerprints. Your number is that of no other; and when your name is called, no one else will hear it. One's final attachment must be with his God in the secret place where no other can enter.

Second: Regardless of how much and how well the conference may stamp the truth on one's mind and heart, the final and only abiding stamp must be placed by the Holy Spirit. Only the anchor of a revealed religion will hold the soul in the storm of life. One must pierce beneath the councils of men, however good, and cast anchor within the eternal. This must be so since the price of discipleship is the willingness to forsake all others to follow Christ. Our faith must rest in the undesertable.

The apostle exhorted, "Be ye followers of me, even as I also am of Christ" (1 Cor. 11:1). Here he is following Christ, so we can follow him.

I Have No Other Duty

In the Book of Ecclesiastes, the world's wisest man scans his lifetime of searching for reality and leaves for us some of his findings. We quote him on a few of his conclusions: "I gave my heart to seek and search out . . . I have seen all the works that are done under the sun . . . I am come to great estate, and have gotten more wisdom than all they that have been before me in Jerusalem . . . I made me great works . . . houses . . . vineyards . . . gardens and orchards . . . trees . . . of all kind . . . I made me pools of water . . . I got me servants and maidens . . . cattle . . . silver and gold . . . men singers and women singers . . . I withheld not my heart from any joy . . . I hated all my labour . . . For all [man's] days are sorrows, and his travail grief . . . I praised the dead . . . more than the living . . . He that loveth silver shall not be satisfied with silver." He adds, "Vanity of vanities . . . all is vanity" (1:13-14, 16; 2:4-8, 10, 18, 23; 4:2; 5:10; 12:8).

Against the background of all of his experiences and his findings through wisdom, he emerges with this timely message to youth: "Remember now thy Creator in the days of thy youth," and ends with these words of supreme wisdom: "Let us hear the conclusion of the whole matter: Fear God, and keep his commandments: for this is the whole duty of man" (12:1, 13).

The "conclusion" of the matter is this important part, and his conclusion was inspired by God. It was reaffirmed by Jesus in His memorable words to one of His much-loved friends: "Martha, Martha . . . one thing is needful" (Luke 10:41-42).

44

In these two statements—the "conclusion" and the "one thing needful"—coming from the two wisest men of the ages, is found the secret of a quiet and peaceful life. The fret, the fume, the furor, the frenzy, and the frustrations of life are swept away, and a single task becomes the sole guiding star for life's journey: Obey God; "I have no other duty."

To some this may seem to be an oversimplification of life's task, but that is not the case. No man ever lived a fuller life than the Nazarene, and yet His life embraced but one task: "I come to do thy will, O God" (Heb. 10:9, 7).

If the doing of the divine will is life's supreme and only necessary task, it follows that to know what the will of God is, is the most important information obtainable. To know His will is the essence of wisdom; therefore it is written, "Be ye not unwise, but understanding what the will of the Lord is" (Eph. 5:17).

Tons of anxiety roll off one's back when he realizes that he has but one duty to perform. Life resolves itself into a search to know it and a will to do it.

Life thus centered becomes oriented. It is drawn into harmony with one's Creator; its purposes spring from His suggestions; its power is drawn from His resources; and its immortality insured by Him "who only hath immortality" to bestow (1 Tim. 6:16).

What a relief to know that one has no obligation or duty that arises from any other source but the divine will. This makes all of life sacred, so "whether . . . [we] eat, or drink . . . [we] do all to the glory of God" (1 Cor. 10:31).

Let it not be thought that the one thus living has no obligation to his neighbor. He has, but this obligation does not arise from the will of his neighbor but from the will of God; hence, it does not bear the feeble strength of man's desire but the authority of the divine power.

Thus all of man's acts are supported by the power of God, for they are of His ordering. In the line of such ordered

45

service, the command is "Let the weak say, I am strong" (Joel 3:10). Why not? He is fulfilling the commands of God and may expect the divine power in doing the will of the Master.

Herein lies the power of the Christian. First comes his orders, followed by the power to execute them. In this context the apostle Paul wrote, "I can do all thing through Christ which strengtheneth me" (Phil. 4:13).

"This is the whole duty of man." What a thought! How simple does it appear! Can one really accept it as fact? It must be true, of course, for the wisest man begotten of man declared it, and the only man begotten of God affirmed it. It must be true whether I believe it or not. Seriously, I am trying desperately to both believe and understand it.

If it is true, I can begin to see wisdom in such divine injunctions as, "Be careful for nothing" (Phil. 4:6); "Fear none of those things which thou shalt suffer" (Rev. 2:10); "Take no thought for your life"; and "Seek ye first the kingdom of God, and his righteousness; and all these things shall be added unto you" (Matt. 6:25, 33).

Thus living, one can see the wisdom of Jesus' manner of life when He affirmed, "I receive not honour from men" (John 5:41); and one can more willingly accept His kind rebuke, "How can ye believe, which receive honour one of another, and seek not the honour that cometh from God only?" (v. 44).

Thus living, the words of Peter, "That he no longer should live the rest of his time in the flesh to the lusts of men, but to the will of God" (1 Pet. 4:2) (spoken of those who have died with Christ and have been raised with Him), take on utilitarian value; in fact, they become the goal of every informed Christian.

In the light of these facts, what is the inescapable conclusion? If only one thing is needful, and that is to know and do His will, it follows without doubt that we must take time with the Master. We must cultivate a knowledge of His voice, gain certainty of His commands, and listen only for His approval. Then, and then only, can we believe.

46

The Heritage of Babes

In the midst of one of His teachings, Jesus paused and said, "I thank thee, O Father, . . . because thou hast hid these things from the wise and prudent, and hast revealed them unto babes" (Matt. 11:25).

Here Jesus is thanking the Father for both the hiding and the revealing. It is not too difficult to understand why He was grateful for the revealing—He had come to reveal truth; but it is more difficult to understand His praise for the hiding.

The answer lies in the nature of those from whom He hid His truth. They were the worldly-wise, those who felt that by their own wisdom and searching they could discern spiritual truth. Their trust was in themselves and not in the Revealer.

Here God places the knowledge of truth completely beyond the pale of such persons. Zophar asked the question, "Canst thou by searching find out God?" (Job 11:7). Isaiah answers, "There is no searching of his understanding" (Isa. 40:28).

By no amount of intellectualism can one come to know God. God has hidden truth from the self-sufficient, and what God hides no one can discover. This explains why some of the world's intellectually great are utterly ignorant of spiritual reality.

Jesus thanked God that He had thus acted. The intellectually self-sufficient have no feeling of dependence upon another; they are "wise in [their] own conceits" (see Rom. 11:25; 12:16), and we are amply warned to stay clear of such:

"Beware lest any man spoil you through philosophy and vain deceit" (Col. 2:8).

The desire to be wise in a wisdom that is not of God was a major in man's original sin, and it has clung to the natural man and is only removed by death to self.

Against such persons God has sealed off His wonderful truth, and Jesus thanked Him for doing so.

On the other hand, God has "revealed them unto babes—the unassuming, the meek, the dependent, the "poor in spirit" (Matt. 5:3). The very fact that truth can come only as a revelation means that the glory of its coming is due to the Revealer. We are utterly dependent upon Him for spiritual understanding. The promise to reveal is unequivocable but conditional, and if the revelation is not forthcoming, the condition has not been met.

"Thou hast . . . revealed them unto babes"—babes that are unassuming, trustful, loving. This condition of the divine revealing must be and is continuous. The revealing ceases when babelikeness ceases.

Jesus added, "For so it seemed good in thy sight" (v. 26). We may never know just why anything seems good in God's sight, but at times He has given us some hints and some reasons.

One reason why God has placed the reception of spiritual truth on the basis of revelation and not intellectual research is so that no one could "glory in his wisdom" (Jer. 9:23). God sees to it that all the strut and pride must be removed from the heart before His secrets can be understood. Pride was one of Satan's sins, and it sprang from his wisdom; so wisdom has been a natural nursery for pride, and pride separates from God. If one by his own tireless efforts, self-development, and mental prowess comes to understand the secret of the Almighty, then he has only himself to praise. He no longer needs God to help him to understand. He has risen to the level of his Maker already. God sees to it that this can never happen; He has "hid" His wondrous truths from such.

Then, too, God seeks the worship of man; and why should man worship a being whose depths of wisdom he could plumb by his own wisdom? He would worship himself instead. God has closed the door to any legitimate worship of the creature and has opened it for the worship of the Creator. Herein His wisdom is seen.

It is the purpose of God to help man to be ever conscious of his position of subservience to his Creator, and He has blocked every entrance to "God-equality"; godlikeness, yes; but equality, never. In "hiding," God keeps man conscious of his position.

The wisdom of God in hiding the deeper things from the natural man is a revelation of His love for us. He is saying to us that He desires that we live with Him eternally, and no one who desires to rise to His level of knowledge and power can live with Him. Satan tried this and was cast out, so that path has been banned. The road to ruin has been closed. Love closed it; it says, You just can't find in your own proud, self-sufficient self; you must realize that your only hope is in a Revealer who reveals alone to babes.

This kind of living was preached to man. But in addition to the teaching, Christ came to exemplify it and to show us that it can work here on earth in a real human being. To do so, He "was made flesh" (John 1:14), took our form, our nature, our humanity, and lived the life of a babe, totally dependent upon the Father—receiving revelations of truth, duty, and guidance from above. In so doing, He showed us the way to spiritual understanding and invited us to follow the pattern of His life and spirit. The glory that He received and the crown that He wears assures us that thus living, we may sit with Him in the heavenlies forever.

It was the vision that He had of having followers who would be with Him forever that prompted Him to rejoice that

His Father was revealing the proper path to His would-be followers. It not only seemed good to the Father; it seemed good to the Son.

Jesus rejoiced in everything that the Father rejoiced in. When we learn to do that, our rejoicing will be eternal. This is the desire of both the Son and the Father; hence the hiding and revealing. It is love made manifest.

The Christian's Rest

What is this "rest" that the writer of Hebrews says remains to the people of God? Is he talking of a rest that comes after this life, or one that should be ours in this present world?

There is a rest, a cessation from labor, that comes only at the end of life. The Revelator tells us: "Blessed are the dead which die in the Lord . . . : Yea, saith the Spirit, that they may rest from their labours" (Rev. 14:13).

However, the "rest" spoken of in Heb. 4:9 is not the cessation of labors spoken of in the above passage. The context of the verse clearly reveals that. Verse 1 tells us that a promise of such rest has been left us, and we are warned not to "come short of it." This could not refer to a rest after death, because one needs no warning about missing *that* rest, for "it is appointed unto men once to die" (9:27); warning or no warning, the Christian will enter into that rest.

Verse 3 clearly indicates that this rest is for this life: "For we which have believed do enter into rest." Verse 6 tells us that those who fail to enter into this rest, fail "because of unbelief." If the rest referred to is the rest after death, neither faith nor unbelief would determine the entrance. "There remaineth therefore a rest to the people of God" (v. 9), and this rest is for this life.

The key to this passage is "his own"; the one who has entered has "ceased from his own works" (v. 10).

The apostle Paul gives us light on this subject. First, he says that he was "in labours more abundant" (2 Cor. 11:23).

51

And almost in the same breath, he speaks of "striving according to his working" (Col. 1:29). Paul had learned the secret of operating by the power of God, for he had ceased from "his own" works.

Jesus set forth the principle and practiced it. He said, "The Father that dwelleth in me, he doeth the works" (John 14:10). The strength of His life was not in himself, for He said, "I can of mine own self do nothing" (5:30); He operated by the power of Another. He was at rest from His own labors; His works were the works of God.

The life that is empowered by Another is a life without strain. One thus operating has cast his cares upon Him, knowing that "he careth for you" (1 Pet. 5:7). "Let us labour therefore to enter into that rest" (Heb. 4:11). This is the "strait gate" that we are commanded to strive to "enter . . . in" (Matt. 7:13).

The danger of failing to enter is caused by unbelief. The fatal example held before us is that of the Israelites, who failed to enter Canaan at Kadesh-barnea. The spies reported that the land was good, but the enemy was too strong, so unbelief of God's Word caused them to fail to go in.

What *is* the unbelief that would cause us to fail to enter into this rest from our own works and enter into the rest of His working? What is it that we would fail to believe? Here are some of the things that cause people to fail to enter.

There is the lack of faith that God will provide the strength that is necessary when the hour of need arrives. We cannot lie down in sleep because we do not believe that He will supply the needed strength and grace. He has promised, "As thy days, so shall thy strength be" (Deut. 33:25), but if we do not feel that strength now, we hesitate to believe it will be forthcoming when needed.

We are commanded to take no anxious thought for tomorrow, but we roll and toss at night, worrying about the future. Reason? We do not believe enough in God's command to rely upon His word. We are like the doubting Israelites who asked, "Can God furnish a table in the wilderness?" (Ps. 78:19).

Another prolific source of unbelief arises from our reluctance to obey. When one obeys immediately, his faith grows because he sees the fulfillment of God's promises, for the fulfillment is based upon one's obedience.

Faith can come only by listening to God, for "faith cometh by hearing, and hearing by the word of God" (Rom. 10:17). When one begins to look at circumstances and conditions, his faith tends to dwindle. When he looks to Jesus, his faith grows and his courage increases.

This glorious experience of resting from our own works and allowing Another to do the works of God in us is available to all of us. "There remaineth therefore a rest to the people of God." It is here for us. God has provided it, and He longs for us to enter into it. He warns of dangers of not doing so.

"Our own works" is our problem. Involved here is a desire to go our own way, which is man's perennial sin. The call is to relinquish all claim to ourselves and in perfect submission to Him, seek His will to know and to do.

One thus dedicated is free from anxiety, for he has no responsibility but to obey. The consequences and outcome are not his concern. He has done his all when he has fully obeyed. The results are chargeable to the one who gave the orders.

Thus acting, our wisdom is set aside and His will sought. No longer do we lean to our "own understanding" (Prov. 3:5). This is a fatal blow to the human pride. It is, in fact, death to self; but such death is the door—the only door—to life.

The wisdom of God often runs counter to our wisdom, and to surrender ours for His is death-dealing.

To understand the joy of living in the strength of Another, free from carking care and corroding doubt, one must experience it for himself. Here an Old Testament exhortation is to the point: "O taste and see that the Lord is good" (Ps. 34:8). To taste is to hunger for more, and to hunger is to be filled.

It all seems so easy and yet it is not, for the injunction is, "Let us labour therefore to enter in." Man's natural and depraved desire to be on his own, the tide of the world's independence of God, and the satanic effort to defeat God's highest purpose in our lives, together make the "labour" necessary; but the rest is available to us on terms we can meet.

To fail is not necessary.

Made like unto His Brethren

I am searching to know "the man Christ Jesus" (1 Tim. 2:5), or as Peter phrased it, "Jesus of Nazareth, a man" (Acts 2:22). Just now I am not seeking to understand the God who could not die, but the Jesus of Nazareth who could die; for it is by the death of a perfect Man that I am to be redeemed (Rom. 5), and I desire to know my Redeemer.

The Jesus I seek to understand is the One who was "made like unto his brethren" and "was in all points tempted like as we are" (Heb. 2:17; 4:15).

I need a Jesus who needed the help of a God who He was not; Someone other than himself to aid Him, Someone more powerful than himself to be with Him. Hence, it is written, "God was with him" (Acts 10:38). More than a traveling companion, He needed, as do we, Someone in Him to empower Him; hence it is written, "God was in Christ" (2 Cor. 5:19). This One, who was with Him and in Him, was greater than Jesus; Jesus referred to Him as being His Father and said, "My Father is greater than I" (John 14:28). No one can be greater than the Infinite, and if the Father is greater than Jesus, as Jesus affirmed, then Jesus was not infinite. Thank God for that, for it opens the door for me to become like Him—but never as the Infinite.

Jesus, like ourselves, needed the power of the Holy Spirit; and it is written that "God anointed Jesus of Nazareth with the Holy Ghost and with power" (Acts 10:38). After the anointing, He had a power that He did not have before, else the anointing was useless; and since this is true, He was not all-powerful before.

He, like ourselves, needed guidance by Another. Hence, it is written that He "was led by the Spirit" (Luke 4:1). I seek to know this One who needed a guide other than himself and needed a power that He did not have before. It is this Man I want to know. The "God-man" concept baffles me. Let the theologians understand that being if they can, but I will settle for the Man Christ Jesus who said, "I can of mine own self do nothing" (John 5:30), and "The Son can do nothing of himself, but what he seeth the Father do" (v. 19).

I am seeking to know the "Son of man," my Savior who prayed not to the God that He was, but always to His Father who was in heaven. He looked to One who was the source of His life, for, said He, "I live by the Father" (John 6:57), and the Father was greater than Jesus, so Jesus said.

Paul seeks to make the relationship between the Infinite —the Father—and the less than infinite—the "Lord Jesus Christ"—in these words: "But to us there is but one God, the Father, of whom are all things, and we in him; and one Lord Jesus Christ, by whom are all things, and we by him" (1 Cor. 8:6).

It is this "Lord Jesus Christ," who said He was not as great as the Father, but through whom the power of the Father has come to us, that I seek to know. He is not the house but the Door—and the only Door—to the Father; hence, I need to know Him, that through Him I may enter into the heavenlies.

To make Christ equal with the Father not only gives the lie to His own words but closes the door to oneness with Him. I can, in a measure, understand the One who said, "I thirst" (John 19:28), who "was afterward an hungred" (Matt. 4:2), and "being wearied . . . sat thus on the well" (John 4:6); but I cannot comprehend the One who "shall neither slumber nor sleep" (Ps. 121:4), and "who only hath immortality, dwelling in the light which no man can approach unto; whom no man hath seen, nor can see" (1 Tim. 6:16).

For the time being, I am concerned with the Door and the Way, and am looking forward to the findings at the end of the Way and through the Door. It comforts me to know that in the end God "hath given him authority to execute judgment also, because he is the Son of man" (John 5:27). The word "because" is significant. The Infinite stands aside and assigns the judgment of man to the "Son of man," who is less than infinite and who "knoweth our frame" experientially (Ps. 103:14), and who was "made like unto his brethren, that he might be a merciful and faithful high priest" (Heb. 2:17).

It is the Christ "of the seed of David" with whom I can become acquainted and of whom I can have an understanding. This understanding is a progressive something; hence, the constant thrill of new insights into the only begotten Son, like whom we are destined to be when "we shall see him as he is" (1 John 3:2). It is wisely added, "And every man that hath this hope in him purifieth himself, even as he is pure" (v. 3).

The finding of Him will not be full and complete in this life. The great apostle Paul was still crying out near the end of his days, "That I may know him" (Phil 3:10). Did he not already know Him? He affirmed, "I know whom I have believed" (2 Tim. 1:12). Yes, he knew Him, but not fully. One approaches that full knowledge all along his seeking life and is ever rewarded with fuller insights that are harbingers of the full revelation beyond this vale of tears.

It is this helpless and utterly dependent Christ who, by listening and obeying, became Lord of all and the Redeemer of the human race. Having wholly relied upon His Infinite Father, He obtained wisdom, understanding, and power to conquer all man's foes and was assigned Lordship of the universe. The Father has "put all things under his feet" (1 Cor.

15:27). He has become Heir of all things. Thus walking, He has opened up for us a pattern of life that will lead to His throne, for following Him, we are to become "heirs of God, and joint-heirs with Christ" (Rom. 8:17). He stooped to our level and met us in our rags; that through companionship with Him here, we might share His riches forever. This was His task, and He performed it perfectly.

Jesus, the Imperfect

The failure to recognize the Babe of Bethlehem's manger as but an ignorant, helpless, undeveloped child who grew and "increased in wisdom and stature" (Luke 2:52) until He became Savior, is to miss the path by which we must needs journey if we are to sit down with Him in His throne, as He has promised we may.

Jesus did not "know it all" while journeying toward the Cross; neither had He proved His absolute obedience until He willingly hung upon the tree. What He did know in life sprang not from an inherent and infinite Godhood, but from instruction given to Him by the Father. This He repeatedly affirmed. Said He, "As my Father hath taught me, I speak these things" (John 8:28); "As I hear, I judge" (5:30); "We . . . testify that we have seen" (3:11); "All things that I have heard of my Father I have made known unto you" (15:15).

The picture given to us of Christ is that He was wholly dependent upon the Father. He was made like unto His brethren in all things; and describing the brethren's relationship to himself, He used the grapevine illustration and pointed out the utter inability of the branch's power to bear fruit, except by a maintained connection with the vine. It is true that in this illustration He represents himself as the Vine—the One who imparts life and fruit-bearing ability to the dependent branches—but He uses it as a parallel to the relationship that He maintained to the Father, from whom He constantly received this flow of life that He supplied to the abiding branches.

To understand the pattern of our Elder Brother's receiving from the Father that He might transmit to the brethren is to lay bare a pattern that we can follow in relationship to the Son.

Jesus represents himself as utterly helpless, a fact that we are loathe to admit, and yet a fact clearly set forth by the inspired apostle when He said of Christ that He "emptied himself" (Phil. 2:7, margin). If we are to get with Christ, we must meet Him on common ground. We cannot join Him when, at the word of His Father, the Creator, He brought the world into existence. That height we could never reach; hence, it was necessary for Him to descend to our level, that we might unite with Him in the upward trek to the heavenlies.

"He became poor" and helpless that He might unite with us in poverty and helplessness, so we could ascend with Him in riches and power, (2 Cor. 8:9).

The basic reason for man's unwillingness to accept Christ's helplessness grows out of his own unwillingness to admit his own helplessness. The struggle to unite with Christ is the fight against our own supposed self-sufficiency. The very nature of sin, the essence of sin, is a desire to be above God; and we hesitate to admit that Christ, the "Jesus of Nazareth, a man" (Acts 2:22) who walked the dirt roads of time, was less than the Father; for, like Lucifer, we desire to be as God. And yet we know that in union with Christ alone we can be saved; and desiring to be saved, we demand that our Savior be equal with Him of whom Paul wrote: "But to us there is but one God, the Father, of whom are all things" (1 Cor. 8:6). We reluctantly admit that the apostle was setting forth the "one Lord Jesus Christ" as the recipient of "all things" and not as the inherent Possessor. For the "all things" were *of* the Father—inherently His—and *by* the Son.

To understand the "of" of the Father and the "by" of the Son is to open the door to the Son's helplessness and utter dependence on the Father, and to point the way—the only way—by which we can unite with the Son; for only at the point of His helplessness can we meet Him. And meeting Him there, we have confessed our own helplessness, the most difficult admission that man has to make; but it is here that we unite with Christ.

Jesus plainly announced, "My Father is greater than I" (John 14.20), and because Christ is not as great as the Father, I can meet Him and be like Him. I am indeed grateful that my Jesus is not as great as God the Father, for of the Father it is said that He "only hath immortality, dwelling in the light which no man can approach unto; whom no man hath seen, nor can see" (1 Tim. 6:16). I can approach His Son, see Him, and be like Him when I "see him as he is" (1 John 3:2).

Did God the Father "learn"? Jesus did: "Though he were a Son, yet learned he obedience by the things which he suffered" (Heb. 5:8). It is further written, "And being made perfect, he became the author of eternal salvation unto all them that obey him" (v. 9). This passage has no meaning if He was always perfect.

His obedience, though perfect, was step by step (and there was never disobedience). The final perfect and complete obedience could not be demonstrated except in its ultimate expression, which was death upon the Cross, and all that that final step involved.

Jesus was limited in His doing by what He saw the Father do, or at least that is what He said; and He did not see all that His Father was doing as He went along. Note the word "seeth." There was progression in the seeing. The revelation of the Father's will came to Him as a continuous revelation. This He made crystal clear when, in amazement, the disciples looked upon what He was doing, and He assured them that "the Father . . . will shew him [Jesus] greater works than these, that ye may marvel" (John 5:20). Note the "will shew." He could not be seeing it already and use such language.

The helpless Jesus is my Man, a Man showing me the way to God by word and by example. He came all the way to me in His human existence. Glory!

61

Ye Do Dishonour Me

(John 8:49)

How may one dishonor Christ? By representing Him as such a person as He denies being. He is often represented as God—equal with the Father, possessing all power and knowledge, performing miracles in His own strength, and doing whatever He desired to do. All of this is a misrepresentation of "Jesus of Nazareth, a man" (Acts 2:22).

When we ascribe to his deity powers that He, as a man, received by faith from the Father, we close the path that He took and follow Him not. How can we, if He acted as God, and not as a man indwelt by God? Paul said "God was in Christ" (2 Cor. 5:19), and I am seeking to get acquainted with the Christ who had God in Him. The Bible clearly teaches that I—a man—may have God in me; but if Jesus had God in Him because He was God, how then may I have God in me, since I am not God?

Not only do I desire to get acquainted with that Christ who had God in Him, but I want to keep in step with Him, for He is the One who died on Calvary for me. God did not die there, because if He did, who raised God from the dead? The One who died saved me, and I want to know Him.

To say that Jesus performed His miracles and lived a sinless life by the strength of His Godhood is to close the door to our following Him in performing His miracles and in living a sinless life.

A very popular response that I get from people upon whom I urge Christian living—living above sin—is, "Oh yes, but *I* am human." In other words, Christ lived a sin-free life because He was divine; and since we are not divine, we can't live above sin, although God reminds us, "He that hath suffered in the flesh [as Christ] hath ceased from sin" (1 Pet. 4:1).

The fact is, Jesus was a man as I and kept from sinning, not because He was God, but because He followed the same rule for sinless living that He has marked out for us. These are His words: "If ye keep my commandments, ye shall abide in my love; even as I have kept my Father's commandments, and abide in his love" (John 15:10). In other words, He was a man, obeying the Father and abiding in His love only because He was obedient, and not because He was God. I can follow an obedient man who obeys because He loves, but I cannot follow one who obeys because He is God.

Again Jesus said, "He that believeth on me, the works that I do shall he do also" (John 14:12). If we say that Jesus did His works because He was God, how then can I follow Him? In fact, we are not—and why? Jesus did not perform His matchless works by the power of an inherent Godhood, but by faith in obedience to the Father's revealed will. He makes that clear in His own words: "The Son can do nothing of himself, but what he seeth the Father do" (5:19). He never acted upon His own. He was limited to what He saw His Father do.

He was an absolutely helpless person. He said, "I can of mine own self do nothing" (v. 30). This is not the picture of an infinite being, doing what He wants to do, but of a helpless human being, totally dependent upon Another.

How do we dishonor Him? By ascribing to Him powers that He denies having. By doing so, we let Him go alone, when He desires for us to follow Him. If He were acting as God, He would be no pattern for me; just forget it—and in a large measure we have! But if He was a helpless man as He said He was, listening to the Father's voice, watching His Father's acts, and by faith obeying His Father's commands, then He opens the path for me to follow.

Our picture of Christ as God, and God's picture of "God was in Christ," are not the same photographs.

Someone, trying to exalt the human Christ before His post-Pentecostal glorification, was saying, "Jesus in His humanity slept on the boat; in His deity He stilled the storm. In His humanity He grew weary; in His deity He raised Lazarus from the dead. In His humanity He had angels minister to Him; in His deity He cast out devils."

I listened and thought (as I do occasionally) and said to myself, "In his humanity Peter denied his Lord; in his deity he healed the lame man. In his humanity, he was rebukable by Paul; but in his deity he raised Dorcas from the dead."

Then take brother Paul. In his humanity he was cast down, but in his deity he cast the devil out of the girl by the riverside. In his humanity he was with the Corinthians "in weakness" (1 Cor. 2:3), but in his deity he raised the boy from the dead who fell from the third-story windows.

By such argument we have three Gods: Jesus, Peter, and Paul. Thus picturing "Jesus of Nazareth, a man," acting as God in His own right and not as a helpless person, utterly dependent upon the Father, we do dishonor Him. This is done in an effort to exalt Him, but the opposite is true.

It is this erroneous conception of the Man of 33 years on earth that cuts us off from following Him. When we see Him acting as God and not as a man utterly dependent upon God and limited by the Father's revelation to Him, we leave the path He takes and go our own human way, since we cannot follow such a God because we are mere men.

We honor Christ when we picture Him as He was—a helpless, listening, praying Son, receiving orders from the Father and doing them in the faith that what the Father asked Him to do, He would furnish Him the power to do. I can follow such a man, for I have the same Father to draw from that He had.

The Christ after Pentecost—made Lord and seated at the Father's side—is another person, a glorified Lord of Lords; but I must follow Him in the sands of time, and He walked such paths. Let's keep the two pictures separate: the Man of sorrows and the Lord of glory.

Humility Is Born of God-Consciousness

We are commanded to "be clothed with humility: For God resisteth the proud" (1 Pet. 5:5). He "giveth grace unto the humble" (James 4:6). When God gives the command: "Humble yourselves in the sight of the Lord," He connects with it the promise that "he shall lift you up" (v. 10).

This humbling, to be meritorious, must be voluntary: "He that humbleth himself shall be exalted" (Luke 14:11). There is a humbling that is imposed from God as punishment: Isaiah tells us that "the high ones of stature shall be hewn down, and the haughty shall be humbled" (Isa. 10:33).

Christian humility—the kind that Christ had—is self-imposed: "Being found in fashion as a man, he humbled himself," and it was for this that "God also hath highly exalted him, and given him a name which is above every name" (Phil. 2:8-9). We are enjoined: "Let this mind be in you, which was also in Christ Jesus" (v. 5).

To be united with Christ in His humility is to share His exaltation. Christian humility springs from oneness with Christ, and the humility of Jesus springs from His union with the Father.

John, the "disciple that Jesus loved," alone tells us of the humble act of Jesus washing the disciples' feet. Without understanding the very heart nature of Jesus, this lowly act would be unbelievable. He, the Master of storm, Healer of leprosy, Raiser of the dead, and Lord of the universe, stoops to wash His followers' feet. Incredible but for the fact that this Jesus is indeed the Jesus that He is—the Humble One.

More important than the washing of the feet is the announced background of this humble act, the controlling atmosphere in which this menial task was performed.

The setting, the occasion, the background of this humble act are significant and add grandeur to it. Jesus was nearing the end of His earthly journey. It was the time when He "knew that his hour was come that he should depart out of this world unto the Father" (John 13:1), that He took the towel. It was the renewed consciousness "that the Father had given all things into His hand" (v. 3) that created the atmosphere for this lowly service. It was the inner certainty "that he was come from God, and went to God" that made this task for Him a shameless service.

It is very important and revealing that this lowly act of service was performed by the One—the only One—who held "all things" in His hands and had a most intimate relationship with the God of the universe. This humble act is significant because it reveals the source of such humble service. One who is clothed in the garments of the heavens is willing to lay aside his garments of earth to render any kind of lowly service that is necessary.

It is well to note that no disciple of Jesus was willing to perform such a task, and that fact cannot be divorced from the fact that they were not sure that they had "come from God" and were going to God.

This important incident in the life of the Master casts a penetrating ray of light into His very heart and points the way to Christlikeness. He taught humility and practiced it perfectly. When He found himself "in fashion as a man," He humbled himself in absolute obedience to the Father and executed that obedience to the nth degree—even unto death.

There was no task in the Father's kingdom too menial for Him to perform. In the household of God of which He is a part, the pots and pans would never go unwashed for the lack of a servant to do them. The bathroom and all of its facilities would be cared for—if by no other, then by Him. He was of that nature, and that nature grew from His oneness with God.

In contrast, the disciples felt themselves too good, their talents too important, their time too valuable, to take a servant's place. Not the Master; He was the "heir of all things" (Heb. 1:2), and the stooping would not hurt Him.

The one who feels himself above any position in God's kingdom is not Christlike. He may be in the Kingdom, and highly regarded by men, but he is "low caste" by the side of the Master. Manmade institutions may crown him, but in the final day "the first" may be "last."

Look at Christ from any viewpoint—from His humble birth to His death as a criminal. Examine His walk among men, listen to His teachings, sum up all the evidence, and the inevitable conclusion will be: Jesus of Nazareth was a man of humility. He stooped to the lowest tasks and mingled with the outcasts of earth. No fact of His life denies this.

In this framework of self-emptying and condescension, the command is given to His followers: "Let this mind be in you, which was also in Christ Jesus." It was this going down that made possible His final exaltation, and that is a universal pattern for all who will reign with Him. "He that humbleth himself shall be exalted" are His words and are meant for all.

There are many who are feverishly reaching up for a crown and a seat by Him in the ages to come who resent the use of the basin of water and the towels, the broom and the brush, the soap and the Sani-Flush, the suffering and the death that form the foundation for the final rewards.

It is for us, as it was for the Christ, the certainty of our oneness with God that produces the humility like His, the willingness to serve in any capacity of His choice, without jealousy, envy, or even a longing for something better. To do

His will becomes the chief concern; the place and kind of service is incidental. When one possesses this spirit of the Master, joy fills his soul, for he has the assurance that He pleases God; and if that is his supreme desire, and he has reached it, happiness is inevitable.

If the mind of the Master possesses us in time, a seat with Him in eternity is assured.

What Price Boldness

Just before leaving His disciples, Jesus was telling them something of the world conditions that would prevail and the suffering that would face His followers: "They shall lay their hands on you, and persecute you, delivering you up . . . into prisons" (Luke 21:12).

He gave them a special promise for such an hour. They were told, when delivered up, "not to meditate before what ye shall answer: for I will give you a mouth and wisdom, which all your adversaries shall not be able to gainsay nor resist" (vv. 14-15).

This is a most wonderful promise, and we should thank Him for it. Just to think that when "brought before kings and rulers" for Christ's sake (v. 12), He will give such wisdom and boldness that the great of earth cannot "gainsay nor resist."

But before reaching out to receive and use such a gift it might be well to ask yourself the question, Am I ready to use such a gift if it were given to me? At first sight it seems wonderful, but what has been the price of its use?

This power in speech was a possession of the Master; how did He fare in the use of it? The priests and the lawyers could not answer Him, and so what did they do? When He spoke against them and they could not answer in words, they resorted to stones and finally to a cross. The officers did not hesitate to admit, "Never man spake like this man" (John 7:46); but since the leaders were condemned by it, they demanded the death of the Accuser.   Soon after the Jews had thought they had silenced both Him and His message by His crucifixion, the promise of boldness given to His followers when brought before rulers for His sake was realized by one of His followers.

Stephen had been brought to trial; and although not an apostle but only a dedicated laymen, he spoke with such convincing wisdom and boldness that "they were not able to resist the wisdom and the spirit by which he spake" (Acts 6:10). When he accused them of being "stiffnecked and uncircumcised in heart and ears," saying, "ye do always resist the Holy Ghost . . . ye have been now the betrayers and murderers" (of Jesus) (7:51-52), that was more than they could take, so they stoned him to death.

He had received the promise of such wisdom and boldness and had used it, and the end result was indeed wonderful: death for his faith, and a vision of the Savior standing to welcome the first Christian martyr.

John the Baptist is another example of fearlessness in preaching. He faced the throng with: "O generation of vipers, who hath warned you to flee from the wrath to come?" (Luke 3:7). He feared not the king, and his rebuke of sin brought him to the dungeon and a headless end. He had the mouth and wisdom and the courage to use it. His name is high on God's scroll.

Just to emphasize the universality of the price for thus speaking, note the words of Stephen to the Jewish leaders: "Which of the prophets have not your fathers persecuted?" (Acts 7:52). This was one of those statements that could not be gainsaid or resisted and with the typical result—persecution or sometimes death.

Jesus not only accused Jerusalem of killing the prophets and stoning those who were sent unto them, and chided the scribes and Pharisees, calling them hypocrites for garnishing the sepulchers of the righteous prophets whom their fathers had killed; but against this sordid background He also spoke

71

of the future: "Behold, I send unto you prophets, and wise men, and scribes: and some of them ye shall kill and crucify" (Matt. 23:34).

James offers encouragement to those who suffer for Christ's sake today: "Take, my brethren, the prophets, who have spoken in the name of the Lord, for an example of suffering affliction, and of patience" (James 5:10).

Prophets who speak in the name of the Lord have not had an easy time. The dens of lions, the fiery furnaces, the dismal dungeons, and the bleeding backs all cry out in language too clear to be misunderstood: "Which of the prophets have not your fathers persecuted?"

Note it is the prophet who speaks "in the name of the Lord" that gets the persecution. From Old Testament days there have been prophets who spoke to please the people. The people wanted "smooth things" (Isa. 30:10), and such prophets gave them what they wanted to hear. They were hail-fellows-well-met. But Paul wrote, "Do I seek to please men? for if I yet pleased men, I should not be the servant of Christ" (Gal. 1:10).

One must be deeply dedicated to God to be given this irresistible "mouth and wisdom." In fact, the dedication must be unto death, for that could result from thus speaking.

Suffering is inescapable if one speaks the truth without fear or favor. "Yea, and all that will live godly in Christ Jesus shall suffer persecution" (2 Tim. 3:12). Note the "all" and the "shall." If you suffer no persecution, you may be in Christ Jesus, but you are not living a godly life—and that is possible. There are many in Christ who are not much like God. They are building with "wood, hay, stubble," and their entire works will be destroyed; yet if they are in Christ they shall be saved, though "as by fire" (1 Cor. 3:12, 15). One cannot be Christlike and escape suffering for Him. "They have persecuted me, they will also persecute you," Christ said in John 15:20—that is, if you are like Me.

Here is an established law: The fearless produce fear in the fearful, and then the fearful seek to destroy the fearless.

Don't reach out your hand for the irresistible "mouth and wisdom" unless you are willing to accept suffering, and even death, that may attend its use.

Be Strong

To be strong is a command of God just as truly as "Be ye holy," and is just as binding as "Thou shalt not steal." The command is "Be strong in the Lord, and in the power of his might" (Eph. 6:10). With this command, as with all others, God provides a way for its fulfillment. He tells us that "the joy of the Lord is your strength" (Neh. 8:10). Since joy is our strength, how may we have joy? That, too, is revealed to us.

In the 15th chapter of John's Gospel, Jesus gives us that wonderful illustration of the vine and the branches, in which He emphasizes the necessity of our abiding in Him. Repeatedly does He remind us of the necessity of abiding and assures us that only as we are obedient, can we abide in His love.

Having emphasized the necessity of abiding and loving unto obedience, He adds, "These things have I spoken unto you, that my joy might remain in you, and that your joy might be full" (John 15:11). He was so anxious that His followers have the strength of joy that He pointed the way to the fullness of it. Said He, "Ask, and ye shall receive, that your joy may be full" (16:24).

This fullness of joy comes not only from our asking and receiving the things asked for, but rather from the proof that we are in such a oneness with the Master that He will give to us just because we ask. It is the assurance of oneness that brings the full joy, for what greater joy could one have than to know that his relationship with the Son is such that the Son would grant his request just because of that standing?

If this fullness of joy results from asking and receiving, and receiving results from one's standing with the Master, the next—and very important—question is, What kind of standing must one possess and maintain to enable him to ask and receive and thus be joyful, and being joyful, be strong?

In His many teachings, Jesus makes this very clear. He tells us that we must abide in Him, and there can be no abiding unless there is obedience to Him. That was the only way that the Son could abide in the Father, and certainly there is no other way for our abiding. Then to be on the plane of asking and receiving, one must not only abide in Him, but as Jesus put it, "If ye abide in me, and my words abide in you" (John 15:7), then you can ask as you will and receive what you ask, and your joy will be full.

To have His words abiding in us does not mean that we can quote Scripture—surely that is good, and we need to know the Word—but it means that we must be constantly sharing His thoughts, knowing what is in His mind, and by acceptance, making it our own.

When on the way to Jerusalem to die, in the Father's will, for man's sin, Jesus was sharing this truth and His plan with His disciples, Peter "began to rebuke him." But Jesus reprimanded him: "Thou savourest not the things that be of God, but the things that be of men" (Mark 8:32-33). Peter didn't have Christ's words abiding in him. If he had been asking, he would have asked for something contrary to the Father's will and contrary to the Master's words; hence, he was not headed toward "fullness of joy" and its resulting strength.

Jesus kept the words of God in His heart. He said, "I know him, and keep his saying" (John 8:55). Again He said, "I speak that which I have seen with my Father" (v. 38). Peter spoke what he had seen with the devil, not the Father; hence, the rebuke.

Jesus had no words to give to men. Said He, "I speak not of myself." In His high priestly prayer, He said to the Father,

75

"I have given unto them the words which thou gavest me" (John 17:8). And again, "Whatsoever I speak therefore, even as the Father said unto me, so I speak" (12:50). And to indelibly stamp this truth on our minds, He added, "I have not spoken of myself; but the Father which sent me, he gave me a commandment, what I should say, and what I should speak" (v. 49). Jesus had God's Word abiding in Him and had the joy of asking and receiving.

How can one span (or at least, narrow) the gap between a Simon Peter, who "savourest . . . the things . . . of men," and Christ, in whose heart the words of God deigned to dwell?

The key to the difference is seen in such statements of Jesus as: "As I hear, I judge"; "I speak . . . those things which I have heard of him"; "I speak that which I have seen with my Father"; and "as my Father hath taught me, I speak these things" (John 5:30; 8:26, 38, 28).

Note the time-consuming words: "heard," "seen," "taught." Jesus kept the words of the Father in His heart, because He took time to hear, to see, and to be taught. This throws light on His frequent retreats to the mountains, His rising a long while before day to pray. "The Father . . . will shew [the Son] greater works" (John 5:20). The "will shew" of the above indicates that the showing was continuous. His instruction was ever going on, and He was constantly being shown things that He did not know, and preaching what He had just recently been taught.

Jesus was not a know-it-all; He was ever learning, so His ministry was ever fresh and authoritative.

To follow in His steps of aloneness with the Father, and of a perfect love, issuing in perfect obedience, is to narrow the gap between a Peter and Christ.

May we choose this way. Amen.

Why Did the Father Love the Son?

This article is written in the light of a divine commission given to Jeremiah thousands of years ago: "to root out, and to pull down, and to destroy, and to throw down, to build, and to plant" (Jer. 1:10).

About half a century ago (the exact date was not noted on the margin of my Bible), the Lord gave the same commission to me. Over a period of months, I wrote out my thinking on some pages and shared them with no one except the late general superintendent, Dr. Roy T. Williams. And they have remained classified material until this day, shared only with perhaps a half-dozen friends.

Soon after writing, I proceeded to carry out my commission. It was the most expensive enterprise that I had ever encountered. As a general in battle at times has withdrawn to lick his wounds, reassess his situation, and decide upon his next move, so I went my way, closing my mouth, and working in a distant field of endeavor.

Many years of normal ministry followed, and then God began to remind me of the commission and to renew its message. Such renewals came June 15, 1971, and March 27, 1972, with other references thereto that were not dated.

The purpose of this article is to "root out, and to pull down, and to destroy, and to throw down" some false conceptions of "Jesus of Nazareth, a man" (Acts 2:22)—misconceptions that keep us from closely following in His footsteps.

Our subject is, "Why Did the Father Love the Son?" I presume if one should ask 100 Christians this question, the most popular answer would be, "Because He was His only begotten Son."

Jesus gives a fuller and deeper answer to that question. Said He, "Therefore doth my Father love me, because I lay down my life, that I might take it again" (John 10:17).

First note the word "Therefore." He is about to give the reasons for such love. There were causes for it, without which the word "therefore" is meaningless.

He is telling us that this priceless love of the Father rested upon, and arises from, two facts.

Fact No. 1: "Because I lay down my life."

There is nothing unique in one's laying down his life. Many have laid down their lives for causes they deemed worthy to die for; and some may have laid down their lives for friends. Such an act represents the highest form of human love. Jesus gave guidance here when He said, "Greater love hath no man than this, that a man lay down his life for his friends" (John 15:13).

When one dies for his friend, he has reached the peak of human love, but there is no redemption in that kind of love. Redemptive love must reach beyond one's friends to his enemies; and until Jesus came, there is no record that anyone had such love. His love was of a higher type. In contrast with human love that might die for a friend, "God commendeth his love toward us, in that, while we were yet sinners, Christ died for us" (Rom. 5:8).

This act of dying for sinners—in fact, dying as a sinner —was the climactic act of the Son's obedience; and the expressed purpose of His life was to obey: "Lo, I come (in the volume of the book it is written of me,) to do thy will, O God" (Heb. 10:7). He reinforced it by saying, "I came down from heaven, not to do mine own will, but the will of him that sent me" (John 6:38).

In other words, Jesus was saying, "Therefore" the Father loveth the Son, because He has yielded full and final loving obedience.

So God loved the Son because He was obedient. Jesus could truthfully say, "I do always those things that please him" (John 8:29).

In fact, this is the only way that Jesus could abide in the love of the Father. He made that clear, saying, "If ye keep my commandments, ye shall abide in my love; even as I have kept my Father's commandments, and abide in his love" (John 15:10).

Jesus asked, "Why call ye me, Lord, Lord, and do not the things which I say?" (Luke 6:46).

No one can live with God unless he has God's love in his heart. And what is that love that is required? John gives us the answer: "This is the love of God, that we keep his commandments" (1 John 5:3). John further says, "He that saith, I know him, and keepeth not his commandments, is a liar, and the truth is not in him" (2:4).

It bears repeating. Jesus could lay claim to the Father's abiding love because of His obedience. It was not that He was God's Son, but that He was God's *obedient* Son, that caused the Father to hold Him in His love.

Fact No. 2: "That I might take it again."

The second statement in the text is significant. Just why should Jesus taking His life again be a cause for God's love? It is because it represented faith in the Father's promise. It had been written of Him: "Thou wilt not leave my soul in hell" (Acts 2:27). Jesus went to hell with a promise from the Father that He would be brought out before His body decayed. He believed the Father's promise, and therefore the Father loved

Him, for "without faith it is impossible to please him" (Heb. 11:6).

Jesus practiced the life that He calls on us to live. He said that if we would lose our lives for His sake, we would save them. If we are willing to be baptized into His death, we will be raised together with Him in newness of life. Our Christian religion is a death-life process. Even God cannot resurrect a sick man. To be resurrected, one must die.

Jesus marks the way and sets the pattern of absolute obedience as the only method by which He or any of us can abide in the Father's love. He also takes the path of obedience in death that promised eternal life and beckons us to follow.

We see His path—it is well marked; and we see Him in His heavenly seat by the Father. He beckons us to follow, and promises us that if we unite with Him in death, we shall be united with Him in resurrection and will be granted a seat with Him in His throne.

Obedience and faith will make this possible for us, as it does for Him.

We would all do well to pray, *Lord, I will obey;* and *"I believe; help thou mine unbelief"* (Mark 9:24). *Amen.*

The Father of Lights

When James refers to God as being "the Father of lights," he is but restating a truth that is presented to us in many ways: Namely, that the Father is the Supreme Being of the universe, and that "every good gift and every perfect gift is from above, and cometh down from the Father of lights" (1:17).

John tells us that "God is light" (1 John 1:5). There are other lights in the earth, but all of them are derived from the Father of lights. While upon earth, Jesus declared of himself, "I am the light of the world" (John 8:12), and further stated, "As long as I am in the world, I am the light of the world" (9:5); but this light of Jesus was not an inherent light but one derived from the Father.

Examine His statements concerning this light that He was, and it becomes perfectly clear that it came from the Father. To His disciples He said, "He that followeth me shall not walk in darkness, but shall have the light of life" (John 8:12). Here He tells them that *light* is the product of *life*. John had already revealed this truth: "In him [Jesus] was life; and the life was the light of men" (1:4).

The life that was in Jesus, producing the light that He was, had come from the Father. Life was not inherent in the Son but given to Him by the Father: "For as the Father hath life in himself; so hath he given to the Son to have life in himself" (John 5:26).

This life that was given to the Son produced the light

that He was; hence both life and light come to the Son from the Father. One could not be given that which he already possessed.

Jesus told his followers, "Ye are the light of the world" (Matt. 5:14). Certainly this light was not inherent in the disciples but came down from the "Father of lights" through His Son to whom He had given this light of life.

James made a very comprehensive statement when he wrote, "Every good gift . . . cometh . . . from the Father." That includes the gifts to His Son as well as those to His sons. For example, Jesus drew all His strength from the Father and stated frankly, "I live by the Father" (John 6:57). Having thus spoken, He said, "So he that eateth me, even he shall live by me."

This helpless Jesus, who said, "I can of mine own self do nothing" (5:30), points the way for us to follow Him from helplessness to power and strength by constantly drawing upon Him for resources for Christian living.

I am thoroughly convinced that the main reason that we as sons of God are not able to "do exploits" for God (Dan. 11:32) and to follow Jesus Christ in His miraculous works as He promised we could, is our inability or unwillingness to become identified with Him in His utter helplessness and total dependence upon the Father. It is characteristic of fallen humanity to desire to be self-sufficient and to deny utter helplessness. But it takes death, death to self, to enable one to become identified with Jesus Christ.

There has been so much false teaching about "Jesus of Nazareth, a man" (Acts 2:22) that people are shocked when you say that He was not equal with the Father. They say that is pure heresy. But if so, it is the "heresy" Jesus taught when He said, "My Father is greater than I" (John 14:28). He was helpless, and He knew it and was willing to admit it. His honesty opened the way for Him to partake of the fullness of the Father, while our denial of utter helplessness blocks the path He walked and robs us of the resources upon which He was able to draw.

The Father, and the Father alone, has all good things and has released them to His Son, who recognized His helplessness and relied upon the Father in childlike faith and perfect obedience. Learning "obedience by the things which he suffered," and finally "being made perfect" (Heb. 5:8-9), He could say, "All things that the Father hath are mine" (John 16:15). In like manner the storehouse of God's abundance is open to His sons who will follow in the path of His only begotten Son.

It is written, "He that believeth on me, as the scripture hath said, out of his belly shall flow rivers of living water" (John 7:38). Here Jesus said He was speaking of things as they would be when the Holy Spirit came, and this did happen on that day; but alas, there seems now to be but a small stream flowing.

Jesus lamented the fact that at His return there would probably be but little, if any, of such power-working faith. He asked, "When the Son of man cometh, shall he find faith on the earth?" (Luke 18:8). The Holy Spirit has not lost His power, nor has Christ withdrawn His promises of miracle-working power; but it is the shallow dedication of His followers that keeps Him from moving through us in earth-shaking power.

The low state of Christianity set forth in the Book of Revelation is upon us. Respect for God is at a low ebb, and faith for spiritual achievement has well nigh perished. When speaking of this sad state of affairs, John was reminded that the worst of the backsliding churches, the Laodiceans, knew it not but thought they were doing well—in fact, claimed to be rich—but they were naked and blind.

The heavens are not impoverished. The Spirit's power has not been diminished. The problem lies with us, but there is no way to solve a problem if those who have it do not recognize it.

This age is soon closing; "the time is at hand" (Rev. 1:3). The powers of darkness are working overtime. May we be awakened to our danger, our calling, and our opportunity. The Lord is at hand. Awake, O sleeper! Gird on the armor for the final battle. Dedication must be full, even unto death, if we are to "reign with him" (2 Tim. 2:12).

The World Cannot Hate You

(John 7:7)

It must have made Jesus' half brothers in the flesh happy when they heard these words, for who likes to be hated? But their ears must have perked up when Jesus continued, "But me it hateth."

What is the solution to these two divergent statements? The answer is simple but revealing: The brothers were not like Jesus. They were *being* and *doing* nothing that would warrant the world's hatred. Jesus was, and He tells us what it was: "Because I testify of it, that the works thereof are evil."

The scribes, Pharisees, and lawyers gloried in their righteousness. They boasted of their long prayers, their gifts to the Temple, and their alms to the poor; but Jesus told them that such was no evidence of righteousness but rather of pride; and thus motivated, they could not "escape the damnation of hell." He had already charged, "Woe unto you, scribes and Pharisees, hypocrites! for ye are like unto whited sepulchres, which indeed appear beautiful outward, but are within full of dead men's bones, and of all uncleanness" (Matt. 23:33, 27).

No wonder they hated Him! He told them the truth, and the world does not want to hear the truth. They reject truth and light; of such Jesus said, "And this is the condemnation, that light is come into the world, and men loved darkness rather than light, because their deeds were evil" (John 3:19).

Jesus kept His light shining, for He was the Light of the World. Their hatred of Him was inevitable; hence He said, "But me it hateth."

The Lord's disciples at this point were also not a hateable group; at best they were following Jesus afar off, as was later demonstrated. But Jesus was working and training and teaching them that He might bring them into such a relationship and oneness with himself that they would be hated, and for the same reason that He was hated; for there can be no deep oneness with Christ while yet escaping the hatred of the world. That is, if Jesus did not lie, for in speaking of their post-Pentecostal living, He said: "Ye are not of the world, but I have chosen you out of the world, therefore the world hateth you" (John 15:19).

After nestling them close to himself just before leaving them, He prayed thus to the Father: "I have given them thy word; and the world hath hated them, because they are not of the world, even as I am not of the world" (17:14).

To make sure that we understand Him, He said, "Remember the word that I said unto you, The servant is not greater than his lord. If they have persecuted me, they will also persecute you" (15:20). The certainty of their persecution would depend upon His persecution. Was He persecuted? The record is full and undeniable. They persecuted Him. So surely His followers will be persecuted if they follow Him closely.

This hatred that His followers of that day knew was not a passing thing. The chopped heads, the shackled feet and hands, the devouring by lions, and the burnings at the stakes declare in no uncertain terms that Christ's followers suffered. Suffering is universal for the totally dedicated Christian, and that for all time. The record is, "Yea, and all that will live godly in Christ Jesus shall suffer persecution" (2 Tim. 3:12)—not *may*, but *shall!* The world is loaded with those who deny the gospel "lest they should suffer persecution for the cross of Christ" (Gal. 6:12).

In clarion tones Jesus sounded the warning that in the last days there would be intense suffering for His followers:

"They shall lay their hands on you, and persecute you, delivering you up . . . into prisons" (Luke 21:12).

"And ye shall be hated of all men for my name's sake" (v. 17).

"Then shall they deliver you up to be afflicted, and shall kill you: and ye shall be hated of all nations for my name's sake" (Matt. 24:9).

Lest we should forget, Jesus adds: "Behold, I have told you before" (v. 25).

Jesus transformed those unsanctified disciples and His brothers to whom He had said, "The world cannot hate you," into fire-baptized holy men and women who met hatred and opposition wherever they went. Unlike the pre-Pentecost believers who "believed on him; but . . . did not confess him, lest they should be put out of the synagogue: for they loved the praise of men more than the praise of God" (John 12:42-43), these Holy Ghost-baptized followers of the Master defied their heathen rulers, saying, "Whether it be right in the sight of God to hearken unto you more than unto God, judge ye. For we cannot but speak the things which we have seen and heard" (Acts 4:19-20).

These fire-baptized men "loved not their lives unto the death" (Rev. 12:11). One of their number, the last apostle chosen, reached out for fellowship in Christ's suffering, saying, "That I may know him, and the power of his resurrection, and the fellowship of his sufferings, being made conformable unto his death" (Phil. 3:10). He had not forgotten what he had written to Timothy: "If we suffer, we shall also reign with him" (2 Tim. 2:12).

As I scan the landscape, I find many, many professed followers of the Hated One who frankly say that they are

87

hail-fellows-well-met and accepted by all, or nearly all. In fact, some argue that such teaching as hatred for Christians is an archaic, irrelevant, and outmoded teaching. Such are those who "crucify to themselves the Son of God afresh, and put him to an open shame" (Heb. 6:6). They know Him not as He is, and have little or no desire to see Him as He is, or to be like Him—"despised and rejected of men" (Isa. 53:3).

I cannot be an honest-minded thinker, and open-eyed observer, a sincere believer in the words of the Hated One and the words of other writers inspired by the Holy Spirit, and in Judgment Day honesty report what I fully believe to be true, and say other than I know but few that I honestly believe live this deeply with the Master. I am the judge of no man. God alone can do that, but I would be a liar should I repudiate the statements of this paragraph.

May God have mercy on me and upon you, should you feel its need. Amen.

I ... Will Put My Words in His Mouth

God has for ages past been putting His words in the mouths of His messengers. Moses was such a messenger of God, and note what God said to him: "Now therefore go, and I will be with thy mouth, and teach thee what thou shalt say" (Exod. 4:12). Moses went with the God-given message, and God backed it up with miraculous power.

The points of emphasis here are that Moses did not have God's message within himself; he must get it from God. Then, too, it is evident that God has the ability to communicate with man, and man is able to know that it is a divine communication.

Take the case of Balaam. He had no divine message of his own. He declared, "Have I now any power at all to say any thing? the word that God putteth in my mouth, that shall I speak" (Num. 22:38). Balaam sought God's message, "and God met Balaam: and he said unto him" (23:4). The message may be read and need not be copied here. The point at issue is that God has the ability to deliver messages to men, messages that they can understand.

Another case is that of Micaiah. When he was called before King Ahab, he said, "As the Lord liveth, what the Lord saith unto me, that will I speak. . . . And he said [to the king], Hear thou therefore the word of the Lord" (1 Kings 22:14, 19). Micaiah had no word from God except as God revealed it unto him. He listened and then spoke.

In Daniel's case, the word of the Lord was revealed unto him. He did not possess it himself. It came from above.

It was a standard announcement of the ancient prophets when addressing the people: "Hear ye the word of the Lord." They had no word of God, except as it was given to them.

The command of God to His spokesmen was, "Thou shalt hear the word at my mouth, and warn them from me" (Ezek. 33:7). Be it remembered that the true prophet had no divine message of his own; he received it and passed it on to others. The Old Testament is replete with instances of men receiving messages from God and delivering them to the people. God has the ability to communicate to all men. In fact, He had the ability to communicate through Balaam's ass. He has not been limited by a single method of communication: "God . . . at sundry times and in divers manners spake in time past unto the fathers by the prophets" (Heb. 1:1).

Although God spoke through the prophets in "divers manners," He always made the message clear, and the true messenger declared it fearlessly. Since it bore the penalty of death for disobedience, it must therefore be clear and unmistakable.

Again, it must be emphasized that no messenger of old had the message within himself. The holy men of old spake as they were moved by the Holy Ghost. The message was a revelation, and the power to deliver it was from above.

While speaking to Moses, God told him: "I will raise them up a Prophet from among their brethren, like unto thee, and will put my words in his mouth; and he shall speak unto them all that I shall command him" (Deut. 18:18).

There is no doubt as to who this Prophet was, for on the Day of Pentecost, Peter, speaking under inspiration, identified Jesus as the Prophet of whom Moses spoke. To give further witness, Stephen, in his valedictory address, identified Him as the Prophet. "God . . . hath in these last days spoken unto us by his Son" (Heb. 1:1-2).

What a prophet He was, this Man of the seamless robe! When messengers were sent to take Him and tarried to hear Him speak, they returned saying, "never man spake like this man" (John 7:46). And when He had finished a matchless address, it was said: "He taught them as one having authority, and not as the scribes" (Matt. 7:29). His enemies were amazed that He was a man of letters, although He had attended none of their schools.

While acclaiming the greatness of His message, and accepting it as a message of God, we are reluctant to believe that like all the other true messengers of God, He had no message of His own. It did not spring from an inherent Godhood, but it was revealed from the Father. Its validity arose not from the fact that it was delivered by Him, but from the fact that it came from the Father. This He repeatedly affirmed. He had no message of His own. Like John the Baptist, who referred to himself as but "the voice of one crying in the wilderness," so the message of Jesus was but an echo of the Voice from above. No higher compliment could be given to His message than to say it was an echo, for an echo is a perfect replica of the original. So Jesus could truly say, "The word which ye hear is not mine, but the Father's" (John 14:24); "Whatsoever I speak therefore, even as the Father said unto me, so I speak" (12:50).

It can be truly said, and proven by repeated words from His own lips, that the message that Jesus spoke sprang not from the latent resources of an infinite Godhood but from the mouth of His Heavenly Father. Like all the other prophets, He could only indicate, I listen to what God tells Me to say; His word, and His alone, is final. "If I bear witness of myself, my witness is not true"; then He added, "The Father that sent me beareth witness of me . . . and I know that the witness which he witnesseth of me is true" (John 5:31; 8:18; 5:32).

So we have *"Jesus of Nazareth, a man"* as helpless as any of the sons of God saying with emphasis, "I can of mine own self do nothing" (John 5:30). I am limited in what I say and do by what I see and hear from My Father, for "the Son can do nothing of himself, but what he seeth the Father do" (v. 19). He spoke what He "heard," and His hearing was perfect, and His speaking a perfect echo of what He heard. "Hear ye him," said the Father.